VELOCITY READING

"When one reads too quickly or too slowly, one hears nothing"

Blaise Pascal

Velocity Reading

VelocityReading.
© 2022 Gilles Lavoie

All Rights Reserved. No portion of this book may be reproduced, stored in any form, or transmitted without the author's prior permission or its publisher.

About the Author

The author learned to read faster and better at 14 years old while attending weekly reading hour at the school library. To enjoy that hour he used his new skill to read a whole fiction book within the period. Today, he often read an entire nonfiction book at the bookstore while waiting for his spouse to pick one to buy.

Dedication

In addition to you, I dedicate this book to parents and teachers that teach kids to learn to read with their love and patience.

Although living, experimenting, is the most effective ways to learn and master anything, reading is a powerful leverage to accelerate the learning process. It provides access to the thoughts and knowledge of individuals that would not be possible otherwise.

Disclaimer

This book offers no representations or warranties of success and disclaims implied warranties. Its objective is to help you acquire better skills at reading. You accept and understand that the author shall not be liable for any consequences, direct or indirect, of you, using this knowledge or skills.

Trademarks

Specific names, words, icons, or other marks may constitute trade names or trademarks. The display of any trade name or trademark in this book does not imply, implicitly or explicitly, that any individual or company associated with this book owns a license of these trade names or trademarks.

"Speed describes only how fast an object is moving. In contrast, velocity indicates how fast and in what direction the object is moving."
            Edwin Bidwell Wilson

"When one reads too quickly or too slowly, one hears nothing."
                Blaise Pascal

"The critical thing is not to read too quickly but to read each book concerned at the speed it deserves."
            Jacques Bonnet, literary critic.

"When one cannot read, one has eyes without seeing."
             Maxime of ancient Greece.

"I had a lot of dreams when I was a kid, and I think a great deal of that grew out of the fact that I had a chance to read a lot"
                  Bill Gates

"Reading is the gateway skill that makes all other learning possible, from complex word problems and the meaning of our history to scientific discovery and technological proficiency."
              Barack Obama

"Books were my pass to personal freedom." "What I love most about reading: It gives you the ability to reach higher ground. And keep climbing."
              Oprah Winfrey

"The most important investment you can make is in yourself."
               Warren Buffet

Velocity Reading

VelocityReading.

*"Speed describes only how fast an object is moving
, whereas velocity gives both how fast and
in what direction the object is moving."*

Edwin Bidwell Wilson

Congratulations!

*Congratulate yourself!
You took the first step
that will improve your life, forever!*

Velocity Reading

TABLE OF CONTENTS

INTRODUCTION 12

.... 14

PART ONE - FOUNDATION 15

LESSON 1. THE TENNIS TECHNIQUE 17

This lesson is the cornerstone of Velocity Reading. 17

LESSON 2. AS IN BADMINTON. 39

Increase the width of your vision while reading. 39

LESSON 3. NORMAL TEXT 57

Practice reading a normal text. 57

EVALUATE YOURSELF 71

It's time to take stock. How you read should have changed a lot already. 71

. ... 74

PART TWO - TOOLS 75

.... 75

LESSON 4. VERTICAL READING TECHNIQUES. 77

Your eyes and your vision are circular 77

LESSON 5. VERTICAL READING TECHNIQUES 2. .. 107

Read several words on several lines on several columns 107

LESSON 6. KEYWORDS SEARCHING TECHNIQUES 143

Find keywords faster and effortlessly. 143
6.1 KEYWORDS SEARCHING TECHNIQUE #1. 143
6.2 KEYWORDS SEARCH TECHNIQUE #2 151
6.3 SEARCH TECHNIQUE #3… 159
SUMMARY 169

What to do with it in your daily life. *169*

LESSON 7. SCANNING TECHNIQUES. **171**

A tool to save time *171*

LESSON 8. SKIMMING TECHNIQUES. **189**

Skimming or the art of extracting "la crème" of a text. *189*
LESSON 8.1 THE X TECHNIQUE 193
LESSON 8.2 THE SPIRAL TECHNIQUE 207
LESSON 8.3 IN COLUMNS 223
LESSON 8.4 THE COIL SPRING TECHNIQUE 237
LESSON 8.5 THE ZIG ZAG TECHNIQUE 253
LESSON 8.6 SKIMMING SUMMARY 263

LESSON 9. WHY WE DON'T SUGGEST THE FOLLOWING TOOLS. **267**

The Finger *269*
The Hand *270*
The Pencil or Pen *270*
Software *271*
Summary *272*

LESSON 10. REGRESSION & SUBVOCALIZATION **275**

Easier solutions than you might think *275*
REGRESSION 275
SUBVOCALIZATION 279
CONCLUSION & OUR RECOMMANDATION 281

LESSON 11. WRAP-UP **285**

Wrap-up of what and how to read better, faster, that you now master. *285*

THANK YOU **291**

We are glad that you took the initiative to learn these skills .. *291*
The competitive environment in which we live is getting more challenging *291*
Share what you learned with the people most important to you *291*

7

Velocity Reading

	292
PART THREE – BONUSES	**293**
	293
LESSON 12. TACTICAL & ADVANCED READING	**295**

How to read a 300-page book within one hour! 295
THE TECHNIQUE 296
12.1 - The Cover Page 297
12.2 - Back of the Book 298
12.3 - Table of Contents 298
12.4. Introduction 301
12.5 Index ... not just to search. 301
12.6 Flip the pages 302
12.7 Scan and Skim the chapters picked in step 3 302
12.8 Read Those Few Chapters You Selected 303
12.9 Take notes. 303
EXAMPLE: OUR TACTICAL READING OF 307
The 7 Habits of Highly Effective People 307
   12.1 Cover Page 307
   12.2 Back of The Book 308
   12.3 Table of Contents (TOC) 309
   What is your interest? 309
   12.4 Introduction 311
   The 7 Habits 311
   12.5 Index 313
   12.6 Flipping the Pages 315
   In comparison 317
   12.7 Scan and Skim the chapters you picked in step 3 ... 318
   12.8 Reading 318
   12.9 How to end 318
   The End 319
GET THE ONLINE VERSION OF LESSON 12 321
It is Over-The-Shoulder Training. You Will See Exactly How I Do It. 321
TIPS ON TAKING NOTES WITH EXAMPLES 323
Icons and diagrams 323
Example of abbreviations 324
Useful comments 324

IF YOU SUBSCRIBE **329**

- *Additional tips* *329*
- *Reminders* *329*
- *free training* *329*

FREE ACCESS 331

- 3 VERY POWERFUL MEMORY TECHNIQUE PRESENTATIONS 331
a. *The Loci Method* *331*
b. *The Peg Method* *331*
c. *The Link System* *331*
- HOW FAST WE FORGET AND THE BEST SOLUTION NOT TO! 331
- IS YOUR DREAM TOO BIG? 331
- A TIME MANAGEMENT TIP 331
- A FEW INSPIRATIONS VIDEOS 331
- SIX MYTHS ABOUT READING FASTER THAT DIE HARD AND THE REALITY. 331

APPENDIX 333

BOOKS USED IN THE LESSONS → LINKS TO FIND THEM ONLINE 333
INDEX PAGES OF THE 7 HABITS OF HIGHLY EFFECTIVE PEOPLE ... 335

FINAL WORDS 339

FRIENDLY REMINDERS 341

- STAY TUNED FOR MORE… 341
- SUBSCRIBE TO RECEIVE TIPS AND NEW COURSES FROM TIME TO TIME 341
- MAKE SURE YOU HAVE **FREE ACCESS TO THE BONUS VIDEOS** 341
- PRACTICE 341
- SHARE 341

Velocity Reading

Velocity Reading

INTRODUCTION

Time and Speed: It's all relative!

This is no ordinary book.
This is a book on how to read other books.
There will be no introduction or a lengthy explanation.
Instead, we will jump right into what you must do.

Main Principle of *V*elocityReading.

Let your <u>brain</u> drive your readings,
not the eyes, the finger, or anything else.

→ **Reading faster is a tool**, not the objective.

It is the **main philosophy**, principle, the basis of *V*elocityReading.

The Objective

Every book's author (even in 600 pages book) has one main idea. Everything else is in line with that key belief.

Find that key. You will save a lot of time. You will know how to relate to and structure everything in the book to learn faster, remember better, and understand better.

Here is the pivotal belief of VelocityReading:

Your mind/brain is the driver, not your eyes!

Let this sink in because it is the most important principle for you to understand.

Let speed come from your brain, asking for "food" and pulling for more instead of you pushing your eyes. That is how you will always use the right reading skill, speed, and techniques at the right time for better learning and understanding.

Velocity Reading

It will serve you the rest of your life!

Enjoy and Have Fun!

PART ONE
FOUNDATION

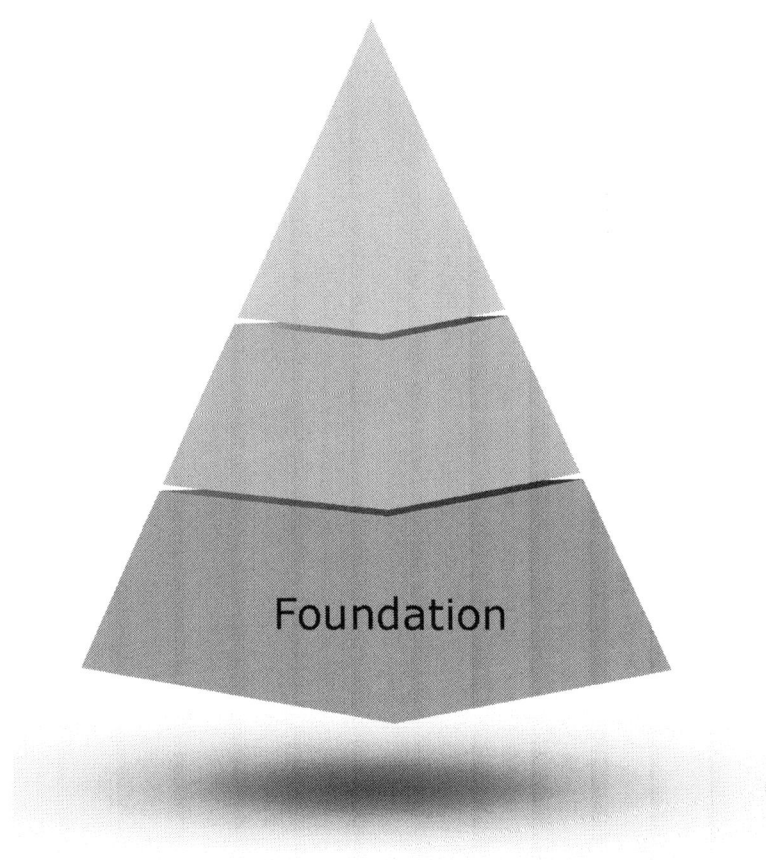

of Velocity Reading

Velocity Reading

_V_elocityReading. Lesson 1. The Tennis Technique

"When one reads too quickly or too slowly, one hears nothing."

Blaise Pascal

LESSON 1. THE TENNIS TECHNIQUE

The analogy is that tennis has three areas to watch:
the service, the landing, and the return.
In this lesson, you will practice reading
with three glances per line.

This lesson is the cornerstone
of VELOCITY READING.

Nothing less.

The objective
Read much faster without skipping any text.
That sums it up. Why complicate?

The key point to improve
Example, when you read the following text:
(Excerpt from the book The Little Prince)

I ask for the indulgence of the kids who may read this book for dedicating it to a grown-up. I have a serious reason: he is my best friend in the world. I have another

Velocity Reading

reason: this grown-up understands everything, even books about children.

If you still read slow, you probably read word by word, like this:

I ask | the | indulgence | of | the | kids | who | may | read | this book | for | dedicating | it to | a grown-up. I have | a | serious | reason: | he | is | the best | friend | I have | in | the world. | I | have | another | reason:| this | grown-up | understands | everything, | even | books | about | children.

It slows you down to read word by word.

The solution

Read more words at the same time.

Learn to read each line of text in two or three steps.

Go ahead and do the first lesson to learn just that.

The Tennis Technique

VelocityReading. Lesson 1. The Tennis Technique

"When one reads too quickly or too slowly, one hears nothing.

Blaise Pascal

Instruction
- Read the following text from left to right.
- Each column is the same text that repeats.
- Try to see each column of text in one glance.
  i.e., three glances per line.

Please go slowly.
Do not try to go too fast.
It's training, not racing.

Do not worry about doing it too slowly at this time.
As your comfort increases,
you will automatically go faster.

Master the technique before the speed.

It is the most effective exercise to increase your speed.

Let your brain and your eyes gain experience and become comfortable.

Learn to see the text of one column's sentence at a glance –three glances per line.

Begin.

Velocity Reading

Beginning of the text

TO LEON WERTH	TO LEON WERTH	TO LEON WERTH

I ask for
the indulgence of
the children who
may read this book
for dedicating it to
a grown-up. I have
a serious reason:
he is my best
friend in the
world. I have
another
reason:
this grown-up
understands
everything,
even books about
children. I have a
third reason: he
lives in France,
where he is hungry
and cold. He needs
cheering up. If all
these reasons are
not enough, I will
dedicate the book
to the child from
whom this grown-
up grew. All

I ask for
the indulgence of
the children who
may read this book
for dedicating it to
a grown-up. I have
a serious reason:
he is my best
friend in the
world. I have
another
reason:
this grown-up
understands
everything,
even books about
children. I have a
third reason: he
lives in France,
where he is hungry
and cold. He needs
cheering up. If all
these reasons are
not enough, I will
dedicate the book
to the child from
whom this grown-
up grew. All

I ask for
the indulgence of
the children who
may read this book
for dedicating it to
a grown-up. I have
a serious reason:
he is my best
friend in the
world. I have
another
reason:
this grown-up
understands
everything, even
books about
children. I have a
third reason: he
lives in France,
where he is hungry
and cold. He needs
cheering up. If all
these reasons are
not enough, I will
dedicate the book
to the child from
whom this grown-
up grew. All

The Tennis Technique

grown-ups were once children, although few of them remember it. And so, I correct my dedication:

TO LEON
WERTH WHEN
HE WAS A
LITTLE BOY.

CHAPTER I

Once when I was six years old, I saw a magnificent picture in a book called
True Stories from Nature, about the primeval forest. It was a picture of a boa constrictor in the act of swallowing an animal. Here is a copy of the drawing. The book said: "Boa constrictors swallow their prey

grown-ups were once children, although few of them remember it. And so, I correct my dedication:

TO LEON
WERTH WHEN
HE WAS A
LITTLE BOY.

CHAPTER I

Once when I was six years old, I saw a magnificent picture in a book called
True Stories from Nature, about the primeval forest. It was a picture of a boa constrictor in the act of swallowing an animal. Here is a copy of the drawing. The book said: "Boa constrictors swallow their prey

grown-ups were once children— although few of them remember it. And so, I correct my dedication:

TO LEON
WERTH WHEN
HE WAS A
LITTLE BOY.

CHAPTER I

Once when I was six years old, I saw a magnificent picture in a book called
True Stories from Nature, about the primeval forest. It was a picture of a boa constrictor in the act of swallowing an animal. Here is a copy of thc drawing. The book said: "Boa constrictors swallow their prey

Velocity Reading

whole, without chewing it. After that, they cannot move and sleep through the six months they need for digestion." I pondered deeply, then, over the adventures of the jungle. And after some work with a colored pencil, I succeeded in making my first drawing. My Drawing Number One. It looked like this: I showed my masterpiece to the grown-ups and asked whether the drawing frightened them. But they answered: "Frighten? Why should anyone be frightened by a hat?" My drawing was not a picture of a hat. It was a picture of a boa constrictor

whole, without chewing it. After that, they cannot move and sleep through the six months they need for digestion." I pondered deeply, then, over the adventures of the jungle. And after some work with a colored pencil, I succeeded in making my first drawing. My Drawing Number One. It looked like this: I showed my masterpiece to the grown-ups and asked whether the drawing frightened them. But they answered: "Frighten? Why should anyone be frightened by a hat?" My drawing was not a picture of a hat. It was a picture of a boa constrictor

whole, without chewing it. After that, they cannot move and sleep through the six months they need for digestion." I pondered deeply, then, over the adventures of the jungle. And after some work with a colored pencil, I succeeded in making my first drawing. My Drawing Number One. It looked like this: I showed my masterpiece to the grown-ups and asked whether the drawing frightened them. But they answered: "Frighten? Why should anyone be frightened by a hat?" My drawing was not a picture of a hat. It was a picture of a boa constrictor

The Tennis Technique

digesting an elephant. But since the grown-ups could not understand it, I made another drawing: I drew the inside of a boa constrictor so that the grown-ups could see it. They always need to have things explained. My Drawing Number Two looked like this: The grown-ups' response, this time, was to advise me to lay aside my drawings of boa constrictors, whether from the inside or the outside, and devote myself to geography, history, arithmetic, and grammar. That is why, at the age of six, I gave up what might have

Velocity Reading

been a magnificent career as a painter. I had been disheartened by the failure of my Drawing Number One and Number Two. Grown-ups never understand anything by themselves, and it is tiresome for children to be always and forever explaining things to them. So, then I chose another profession and learned to pilot airplanes. I have flown a little over all parts of the world; geography has been advantageous to me. At a glance, I can distinguish China from Arizona. If one gets lost in the night, such knowledge is valuable. In this

been a magnificent career as a painter. I had been disheartened by the failure of my Drawing Number One and Number Two. Grown-ups never understand anything by themselves, and it is tiresome for children to be always and forever explaining things to them. So, then I chose another profession and learned to pilot airplanes. I have flown a little over all parts of the world; geography has been advantageous to me. At a glance, I can distinguish China from Arizona. If one gets lost in the night, such knowledge is valuable. In this

been a magnificent career as a painter. I had been disheartened by the failure of my Drawing Number One and Number Two. Grown-ups never understand anything by themselves, and it is tiresome for children to be always and forever explaining things to them. So, then I chose another profession and learned to pilot airplanes. I have flown a little over all parts of the world; geography has been advantageous to me. At a glance, I can distinguish China from Arizona. If one gets lost in the night, such knowledge is valuable. In this

The Tennis Technique

life, I have had many encounters with many people who have been concerned with matters of consequence. I have lived a great deal among grown-ups. I have seen them intimately, close at hand. And that hasn't much improved my opinion of them. Whenever I met one of them who seemed to me at all clear-sighted, I tried the experiment of showing him my Drawing Number One, which I have always kept. I would try to find out if this person was adequately understood. But whoever it was, they would always say: "That is a

Velocity Reading

hat." Then I would never talk to that person about boa constrictors, ancient forests, or stars. I would bring myself down to his level. I would speak to him about the bridge, golf, politics, and neckties. And the grown-up would be exceptionally pleased to have met such a sensible man.

CHAPTER II

So, I lived my life alone, without anyone I could talk to until I had an accident with my plane in the Desert of Sahara six years ago. Something broke in my engine. And as I had with me

hat." Then I would never talk to that person about boa constrictors, ancient forests, or stars. I would bring myself down to his level. I would speak to him about the bridge, golf, politics, and neckties. And the grown-up would be exceptionally pleased to have met such a sensible man.

CHAPTER II

So, I lived my life alone, without anyone I could talk to, until I had an accident with my plane in the Desert of Sahara, six years ago. Something broke in my engine. And as I had with me

hat." Then I would never talk to that person about boa constrictors, ancient forests, or stars. I would bring myself down to his level. I would speak to him about the bridge, golf, politics, and neckties. And the grown-up would be exceptionally pleased to have met such a sensible man.

CHAPTER II

So, I lived my life alone, without anyone I could talk to until I had an accident with my plane in the Desert of Sahara six years ago. Something broke in my engine. And as I had with me

The Tennis Technique

neither a mechanic nor any passengers, I set myself to attempt the complex repairs all alone.

Take a break. Look elsewhere for a few moments.

It was a question of life or death for me: I had scarcely enough drinking water to last a week. I slept on the sand the first night, a thousand miles from any human habitation. I was more isolated than a shipwrecked sailor on a raft in the middle of the ocean. Thus, you can imagine my amazement at sunrise when an

---

neither a mechanic nor any passengers, I set myself to attempt the complex repairs all alone.

Take a break. Look elsewhere for a few moments.

It was a question of life or death for me: I had scarcely enough drinking water to last a week. I slept on the sand the first night, a thousand miles from any human habitation. I was more isolated than a shipwrecked sailor on a raft in the middle of the ocean. Thus, you can imagine my amazement at sunrise when an

---

neither a mechanic nor any passengers, I set myself to attempt the complex repairs all alone.

Take a break. Look elsewhere for a few moments.

It was a question of life or death for me: I had scarcely enough drinking water to last a week. I slept on the sand the first night, a thousand miles from any human habitation. I was more isolated than a shipwrecked sailor on a raft in the middle of the ocean. Thus, you can imagine my amazement at sunrise when an

Velocity Reading

odd little voice awakened me. It said: "If you please--draw me a sheep!" "What!" "Draw me a sheep!" I jumped to my feet, completely dumbfounded. I blinked my eyes hard. I looked carefully all around me. And I saw a most extraordinary small person standing there examining me with great seriousness. Here you may see the best portrait that, later, I was able to make of him. But my drawing is indeed very much less charming than its model. That, however, is not my fault. The grown-ups discouraged me in

odd little voice awakened me. It said: "If you please--draw me a sheep!" "What!" "Draw me a sheep!" I jumped to my feet, completely dumbfounded. I blinked my eyes hard. I looked carefully all around me. And I saw a most extraordinary small person standing there examining me with great seriousness. Here you may see the best portrait that, later, I was able to make of him. But my drawing is indeed very much less charming than its model. That, however, is not my fault. The grown-ups discouraged me in

odd little voice awakened me. It said: "If you please--draw me a sheep!" "What!" "Draw me a sheep!" I jumped to my feet, completely dumbfounded. I blinked my eyes hard. I looked carefully all around me. And I saw a most extraordinary small person standing there examining me with great seriousness. Here you may see the best portrait that, later, I was able to make of him. But my drawing is indeed very much less charming than its model. That, however, is not my fault. The grown-ups discouraged me in

The Tennis Technique

my painter's career when I was six years old, and I never learned to draw anything except boas from the outside and boas from the inside. Now I stared at this sudden apparition with my eyes, somewhat starting my head in astonishment. Remember, I had crashed a thousand miles from any inhabited region in the desert. And yet my little man seemed neither to be straying uncertainly among the sands nor fainting from fatigue, hunger, thirst, or fear. Nothing about him suggested a child lost in the middle of the desert, a thousand miles

Velocity Reading

from any human habitation. When I finally spoke, I said to him: "But--what are you doing here?" And in answer, he repeated, very slowly, as if he were speaking of a matter of great consequence: "If you please--draw me a sheep . . ." When a mystery is too overpowering, one dares not disobey. Absurd as it might seem, a thousand miles from any human habitation and in danger of death, I took a sheet of paper and my fountain pen out of my pocket. But then I remembered how my studies had been concentrated on geography, history, arithmetic,

The Tennis Technique

and grammar, and I told the little chap (a little crossly, too) that I did not know how to draw. He answered me: "That doesn't matter. Draw me a sheep..." But I had never drawn a sheep. So, I drew for him one of the two pictures I had drawn so often. It was that of the boa constrictor from the outside. And I was astounded to hear the little fellow greet it with, "No, no, no! I do not want an elephant inside a boa constrictor. A boa constrictor is very dangerous, and an elephant is very cumbersome. Where I live, everything is tiny. What I need is a sheep. Draw me a

and grammar, and I told the little chap (a little crossly, too) that I did not know how to draw. He answered me: "That doesn't matter. Draw me a sheep..." But I had never drawn a sheep. So, I drew for him one of the two pictures I had drawn so often. It was that of the boa constrictor from the outside. And I was astounded to hear the little fellow greet it with, "No, no, no! I do not want an elephant inside a boa constrictor. A boa constrictor is very dangerous, and an elephant is very cumbersome. Where I live, everything is tiny. What I need is a sheep. Draw me a

and grammar, and I told the little chap (a little crossly, too) that I did not know how to draw. He answered me: "That doesn't matter. Draw me a sheep..." But I had never drawn a sheep. So, I drew for him one of the two pictures I had drawn so often. It was that of the boa constrictor from the outside. And I was astounded to hear the little fellow greet it with, "No, no, no! I do not want an elephant inside a boa constrictor. A boa constrictor is very dangerous, and an elephant is very cumbersome. Where I live, everything is tiny. What I need is a sheep. Draw me a

Velocity Reading

sheep." So, then I made a drawing. He looked at it carefully; then he said: "No. This sheep is already very sickly. Make me another." So, I made another drawing. My friend smiled gently and indulgently. "You see yourself," he said, "that this is not a sheep. This is a ram. It has horns." So, then I did my drawing over once more. But it was rejected too, just like the others. "This one is too old. I want a sheep that will live a long time." By this time, my patience was exhausted because I was in a hurry to start taking my engine apart. So, I tossed off this

The Tennis Technique

drawing. And I threw out an explanation with it. "This is only his box. The sheep you asked for is inside." I was astonished to see a light break over the face of my young judge: "That is exactly how I wanted it! Do you think this sheep will have to have a great deal of grass?" "Why?" "Because where I live, everything is minimal..." "There will surely be enough grass for him," I said. "It is a very small sheep that I have given you." He bent his head over the drawing. "Not so small that-- Look! He has gone to sleep..." And that is how I made

Velocity Reading

the acquaintance of the little prince.   the acquaintance of the little prince.   the acquaintance of the little prince.

End of text

To do
Do the above exercise several times over the next few days.

This is the **most helpful** exercise among all the Velocity Reading techniques. It provides the best and strongest basis to read faster **without skipping any text**.

Practice seeing several words at once.
Practice will make the exercise easier.
Reading faster **and** better is the result we are looking for.
It usually doubles or triples your reading speed **effortlessly**.
Practice several times over the next few days. Make this small investment now.

It will give you a considerable return on investment.

The Objective was:

Double your speed when reading.

What You Learned
- You reduced the number of glances per line.
- You increased your reading speed *effortlessly*.

The Tennis Technique

And most importantly:

You learned to let your brain drive your eyes, not the other way around.

Remember: **speed is a tool, not the objective.**

Why do you read faster than before?

In elementary school, you have learned to read word for word. Consequently, for most of us, it meant up to 7 and 9 eye stops per line.

Why is it a problem?

The eye must stop to read.
Probably, nobody ever told you that.
Eyes do not see well when they are in motion.
Each stop requires time.
Fewer stops = time saved.
Also, your view span is wider than a single word.
It can read more than one at a time. Example:

> The train goes fast

can be read with one glance.

And this is the most effective exercise to understand better whatever you read, while you read faster.

Velocity Reading

Because, when one reads faster, the brain remains concentrated. You will daydream less.

Recommendation

Do this exercise several times to practice reading several words at once.

Practice with your own documents.

Also, practice again with the text above because...

- In this lesson, your brain becomes impatient reading the same text three times.
- You will tend to accelerate naturally and effortlessly. That is the purpose of this lesson:
- **Get your brain <u>to want</u> to read faster**

Letting your mind drive is much more powerful.
You will understand better and remember more.

Practice will make you more comfortable.
Not pushing your eyes will be less tiring.

Learn to let your brain dictate your reading speed.

The Tennis Technique

Velocity Reading

The Badminton Technique

VelocityReading. Lesson 2. Badminton

"Reading is not an easy act. It requires commitment, solitude, attention, curiosity, and a disposition of mind."

Michel Deon

LESSON 2. AS IN BADMINTON.

The analogy to badminton is that there are only two places to look to follow the game. There is the service and the return. In this lesson, you will practice reading with two glances per line.

INCREASE THE WIDTH OF YOUR VISION WHILE READING.

The objective
Increase your ability to read a line with fewer stops.

Instruction
- Read the text from left to right.
- You will notice the same text written twice on the same line.
- Try to see and read each column in one glance. i.e., **two** glances per line.
-

    It will be easier if you **do not read too closely**. Experiment at what distance you should put the text for comfort and ease to view enough text.

39

Velocity Reading

Again...
Please proceed **slowly** at the beginning.
Do not try to go too fast.
This is training, not racing.
Do not worry about doing it too slowly.
As your comfort increases, automatically, you will go faster.

Master the technique before speed.

Again, let your brain and your eye gain experience and get used to it.
Try to see the text of a column's sentence at a glance—two glances per line.

Begin.
Beginning of the text

If you read on a screen, you need to see two columns of text.

TO LEON WERTH	TO LEON WERTH
I ask for the indulgence of the children who may read this book for dedicating it	I ask for the indulgence of the children who may read this book for dedicating it

The Badminton Technique

to a grown-up. I have a
severe reason:
He is the best friend I
have in the world. I
have another reason:
this grown-up
understands
everything,
even books about
children. I have
a third reason:
he lives in France
where
He is hungry and cold.
He needs cheering up.
If all these reasons are
not enough, I will
dedicate the book to
the child from whom
this grown-up grew.
All grown-ups were
once children--
although few of them
remember it. And so, I
correct my dedication:

TO LEON WERTH
WHEN HE WAS A
LITTLE BOY.

to a grown-up. I have a
severe reason:
He is the best friend I
have in the world. I
have another reason:
this grown-up
understands
everything, even books
about
children. I have
a third reason:
he lives in France
where
He is hungry and cold.
He needs cheering up.
If all these reasons are
not enough, I will
dedicate the book to
the child from whom
this grown-up grew.
All grown-ups were
once children--
although few of them
remember it. And so, I
correct my dedication:

TO LEON WERTH
WHEN HE WAS A
LITTLE BOY.

Velocity Reading

CHAPTER I

Once when I was
six years old, I saw
a magnificent picture
in a book called True
Stories from
Nature, about
the primeval forest. It
was a picture of a
boa constrictor in the
act of swallowing an
animal. Here is a copy
of the drawing. The
book said: "Boa
constrictors swallow
their prey whole,
without chewing it.
After that, they cannot
move
and sleep through the
six months they need
for digestion."
I pondered deeply,
then, over the
adventures of the
jungle. And after

CHAPTER I

Once when I was
six years old, I saw
a magnificent picture
in a book called True
Stories from
Nature, about
the primeval forest. It
was a picture of a
boa constrictor in the
act of swallowing an
animal. Here is a copy
of the drawing. The
book said: "Boa
constrictors swallow
their prey whole,
without chewing it.
After that, they cannot
move
and sleep through the
six months they need
for digestion."
I pondered deeply,
then, over the
adventures of the
jungle. And after

The Badminton Technique

some work with a
colored pencil, I
succeeded in making
my first drawing. My
Drawing Number One.

It looked like this: I
showed my
masterpiece to the
grown-ups and asked
whether the drawing
frightened them. But
they answered:
"Frighten? Why should
anyone be frightened
by a hat?"
My drawing was not a
picture of a hat.
It was a picture of a
boa constrictor
digesting an elephant.
But since the grown-
ups could not
understand it, I made
another drawing: I
drew the inside of a
boa constrictor so that
the grown-ups could
see it. They always

some work with a
colored pencil, I
succeeded in making
my first drawing. My
Drawing Number One.

It looked like this: I
showed my
masterpiece to the
grown-ups and asked
whether the drawing
frightened them. But
they answered:
"Frighten? Why should
anyone be frightened
by a hat?"
My drawing was not a
picture of a hat.
It was a picture of a
boa constrictor
digesting an elephant.
But since the grown-
ups could not
understand it, I made
another drawing: I
drew the inside of a
boa constrictor so that
the grown-ups could
see it. They always

Velocity Reading

need to have things explained. My Drawing Number Two looked like this: The grown-ups' response, this time, was to advise me to lay aside my drawings of boa constrictors, whether from the inside or the outside, and devote myself to geography, history, arithmetic, and grammar. That is why, at the age of six, I gave up what might have been a magnificent career as a painter. I had been disheartened by the failure of Drawing Number One and Number Two. Grown-ups never understand anything by themselves, and it is tiresome for children to be always and forever explaining things to them. So, then I chose

need to have things explained. My Drawing Number Two looked like this: The grown-ups' response, this time, was to advise me to lay aside my drawings of boa constrictors, whether from the inside or the outside, and devote myself to geography, history, arithmetic, and grammar. That is why, at the age of six, I gave up what might have been a magnificent career as a painter. I had been disheartened by the failure of Drawing Number One and Number Two. Grown-ups never understand anything by themselves, and it is tiresome for children to be always and forever explaining things to them. So, then I chose

The Badminton Technique

another profession and learned to pilot airplanes. I have flown a little over all parts of the world; geography has been advantageous to me. At a glance, I can distinguish China from Arizona. If one gets lost in the night, such knowledge is valuable. In this life, I have had many encounters with many people who have been concerned with matters of consequence. I have lived a great deal among grown-ups. I have seen them intimately, close at hand. And that hasn't much improved my opinion of them. Whenever I met one of them who seemed to me at all clear-sighted, I tried the experiment of

another profession and learned to pilot airplanes. I have flown a little over all parts of the world; geography has been advantageous to me. At a glance, I can distinguish China from Arizona. If one gets lost in the night, such knowledge is valuable. In this life, I have had many encounters with many people who have been concerned with matters of consequence. I have lived a great deal among grown-ups. I have seen them intimately, close at hand. And that hasn't much improved my opinion of them. Whenever I met one of them who seemed to me at all clear-sighted, I tried the experiment of

Velocity Reading

showing him my Drawing Number One, which I have always kept. I would try to find out if this person was adequately understood. But whoever it was, they would always say: "That is a hat." So then, I would never talk to that person about boa constrictors, ancient forests, or stars. Instead, I would bring myself down to his level.
I would talk to him about the bridge, golf, politics, and neckties. And the grown-up would be exceptionally pleased to have met such a sensible man.

showing him my Drawing Number One, which I have always kept. I would try to find out if this person was adequately understood. But whoever it was, they would always say: "That is a hat." So then, I would never talk to that person about boa constrictors, ancient forests, or stars. Instead, I would bring myself down to his level.
I would talk to him about the bridge, golf, politics, and neckties. And the grown-up would be exceptionally pleased to have met such a sensible man.

CHAPTER II

So, I lived alone, without anyone I could talk to, until I had an accident with my plane in the Desert Sahara six years ago. Something broke in my engine. And as I had with me neither a mechanic nor any passengers, I set myself to attempt the complex repairs all alone.

Take a break. Look elsewhere for a few seconds.

It was a question of life or death for me:
I had scarcely enough drinking water to last a

CHAPTER II

So, I lived alone, without anyone I could talk to, until I had an accident with my plane in the Desert Sahara six years ago. Something broke in my engine. And as I had with me neither a mechanic nor any passengers, I set myself to attempt the complex repairs all alone.

Take a break. Look elsewhere for a few seconds.

It was a question of life or death for me:
I had scarcely enough drinking water to last a

Velocity Reading

week. I slept on the sand the first night, a thousand miles from any human habitation. I was more isolated than a shipwrecked sailor on a raft in the middle of the ocean. Thus, you can imagine my amazement at sunrise when an odd little voice awakened me. It said: "If you please--draw me a sheep!" "What!" "Draw me a sheep!" I jumped to my feet, completely dumbfounded. I blinked my eyes hard. I looked carefully all around me. And I saw a most extraordinary small person standing there examining me with great seriousness. Here you may see the best portrait that, later, I was able to make of

The Badminton Technique

him. But my drawing is indeed very much less charming than its model. That, however, is not my fault. The grown-ups discouraged me in my painter's career when I was six years old, and I never learned to draw anything except boas from the outside and boas from the inside. Now I stared at this sudden apparition with my eyes, somewhat starting my head in astonishment. Remember, I had crashed a thousand miles from any inhabited region in the desert. And yet my little man seemed neither to be straying uncertainly among the sands nor fainting from fatigue, hunger, thirst, or fear. Nothing about

him. But my drawing is indeed very much less charming than its model. That, however, is not my fault. The grown-ups discouraged me in my painter's career when I was six years old, and I never learned to draw anything except boas from the outside and boas from the inside. Now I stared at this sudden apparition with my eyes, somewhat starting my head in astonishment. Remember, I had crashed a thousand miles from any inhabited region in the desert. And yet my little man seemed neither to be straying uncertainly among the sands nor fainting from fatigue, hunger, thirst, or fear. Nothing about

Velocity Reading

him suggested a child
lost in the middle
of the desert, a
thousand miles from
any human habitation.
When I finally spoke, I
said to him: "But--
what are you doing
here?" And in answer,
he repeated, very
slowly, as if
he was speaking of a
matter of great
consequence: "If you
please--draw me
a sheep . . ." When a
mystery is too
overpowering, one
dares not disobey.
Absurd as it might
seem to me, a thousand
miles from any human
habitation and in
danger of death,
I took out of my pocket
a sheet of paper and
my fountain pen. But
then I remembered
how my studies had

him suggested a child
lost in the middle
of the desert, a
thousand miles from
any human habitation.
When I finally spoke, I
said to him: "But--
what are you doing
here?" And in answer,
he repeated, very
slowly, as if
he was speaking of a
matter of great
consequence: "If you
please--draw me
a sheep . . ." When a
mystery is too
overpowering, one
dares not disobey.
Absurd as it might
seem to me, a thousand
miles from any human
habitation and in
danger of death,
I took out of my pocket
a sheet of paper and
my fountain pen. But
then I remembered
how my studies had

The Badminton Technique

been concentrated on
geography, history,
arithmetic, and
grammar, and I told the
little chap (a little
crossly, too) that I did
not know how to draw.
He answered
me: "That doesn't
matter. Draw me a
sheep . . ." But I had
never drawn a sheep.
So, I drew for him one
of the two pictures I
had drawn so often. It
was that of the boa
constrictor from the
outside. And I was
astounded to hear the
little fellow greet it
with, "No, no, no!
I do not want an
elephant inside a boa
constrictor. A boa
constrictor is very
dangerous, and an
elephant is very
cumbersome. Where I
live, everything is very

been concentrated on
geography, history,
arithmetic, and
grammar, and I told the
little chap (a little
crossly, too) that I did
not know how to draw.
He answered
me: "That doesn't
matter. Draw me a
sheep . . ." But I had
never drawn a sheep.
So, I drew for him one
of the two pictures I
had drawn so often. It
was that of the boa
constrictor from the
outside. And I was
astounded to hear the
little fellow greet it
with, "No, no, no!
I do not want an
elephant inside a boa
constrictor. A boa
constrictor is very
dangerous, and an
elephant is very
cumbersome. Where I
live, everything is very

Velocity Reading

small. What I need is a sheep. Draw me a sheep." So, then I made a drawing. He looked at it carefully; then he said: "No. This sheep is already very sickly. Make me another." So, I made another drawing. My friend smiled gently and indulgently. "You see yourself," he said, "that this is not a sheep. This is a ram. It has horns." So, then I did my drawing over once more. But it was rejected too, just like the others. "This one is too old. I want a sheep that will live a long time." By this time, my patience was exhausted because I was in a hurry to start taking my engine apart. So, I tossed off this drawing. And I

small. What I need is a sheep. Draw me a sheep." So, then I made a drawing. He looked at it carefully; then he said: "No. This sheep is already very sickly. Make me another." So, I made another drawing. My friend smiled gently and indulgently. "You see yourself," he said, "that this is not a sheep. This is a ram. It has horns." So, then I did my drawing over once more. But it was rejected too, just like the others. "This one is too old. I want a sheep that will live a long time." By this time, my patience was exhausted because I was in a hurry to start taking my engine apart. So, I tossed off this drawing. And I threw out an explanation with it. "This is only his box. The sheep you asked for is inside." I was astonished to see a light break over the face of my young judge: "That is exactly how I wanted it! Do you think this sheep will have to have a great deal of grass?" "Why?" "Because where I live, everything is very small . . ." "There will surely be enough grass for him," I said. "It is a very small sheep that I have given you." He bent his head over the drawing. "Not so small that--Look! He has gone to sleep . . ." And that is how I made the acquaintance of the little prince.

Velocity Reading

End of text
_____

To do
Do the above exercise again a few times over the next few days.

It helps you to see more words at once.
If you find it difficult, do not be discouraged.

As you get more familiar with its content, the exercise gets easier.

Try putting the text at different distances from your eyes. (Something between 12 "to 18") You may be reading too closely.

The Objective Was
Increase your ability to read a line with fewer stops.

What You Learned
- You accustomed your eyes to reading *much broader*.
- Without even realizing it, you probably often set your eyes on the most crucial word of each sentence as the anchor.

The Badminton Technique

Explanations
The eyes focus on one or two words, and the others on their left and right are a little blurry.

However, you will have noticed several natural reactions that you have developed:

1) You tend to locate the essential words in the sentence and to read these mainly.
2) You often "guessed" the words around in your peripheral vison. However, in practice, your brain sees and reads them even if they are a little fuzzy.
3) You easily accelerated because you already know the text in the right column.
4) Your brain wants more information and faster.

Note
You probably found the exercise a little more complicated. If you have not done well on the entire text. Don't worry. It gets better with practice. It is a complement to Lesson 1.

Reducing the number of glances to three per line is excellent.

To reduce it to two is a plus, but it is most comfortable when you read often.

If you do read often, it will become natural.
If you're occasionally reading, do not worry about it; rely mainly on three stops per line.

Be reasonable. Adjust your expectation to what makes sense.

Velocity Reading

Recommendation
Do this exercise several times. These are the same benefits as lesson 1, but it pushes you further.

Practice using the above text because:

Your brain becomes impatient having to read the same thing several times. You then tend to accelerate naturally and effortlessly.

With practice, you will be more comfortable and keep your brain to be the boss when reading. It is better when your brain leads, not your eyes, tools, or tricks.

It will be more effective for understanding and memory when your brain is leading, hungry for information.

*V*elocityReading. Lesson 3. Normal Text

When asked how he learned to build rockets, Elon Musk said,
"I read books."

LESSON 3. NORMAL TEXT.

PRACTICE READING A NORMAL TEXT.

The objective
To practice on a standard text.

Instruction
Try to read the text in 3 glances.
You have learned to see a little wider.

**Intentionally start reading each new line
from the second or third word of the line.**
You do not need to start from the first word of each line.
You will see it anyway.

As in all previous exercises: slowly at first.
Let your brain and your eye gain experience; get used to it.

Begin

Velocity Reading

Beginning of the text

TO LEON WERTH

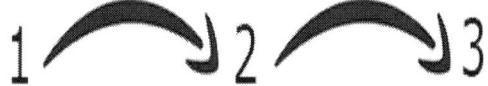

I ask for the indulgence of the children who may read this book for dedicating it to a grown-up. I have a serious reason: he is my best friend in the world. I have another reason: this grown-up understands everything, even books about children. I have a third reason: he lives in France, where he is hungry and cold. He needs cheering up. If all these reasons are not enough, I will dedicate the book to the child from whom this grown-up grew. All grown-ups were once children--although few of them remember it. And so, I correct my dedication:

TO LEON WERTH, WHEN HE WAS A LITTLE BOY

CHAPTER 1

Once when I was six years old, I saw a magnificent picture in a book called True Stories from Nature about the primeval forest. It was a picture of a boa constrictor in the act of swallowing an animal. Here is a copy of the drawing.
The book said: "Boa constrictors swallow their prey whole, without chewing it. After that, they cannot move and sleep through the six months they need for digestion."

I pondered deeply, then, over the adventures of the jungle. And after some work with a colored pencil, I succeeded in

making my first drawing. My Drawing Number One. It looked something like this:
I showed my masterpiece to the grown-ups and asked whether the drawing frightened them.
But they answered: "Frighten? Why should anyone be frightened by a hat?"

My drawing was not a picture of a hat. It was a picture of a boa constrictor digesting an elephant. But since the grown-ups could not understand it, I made another drawing: I drew the inside of a boa constrictor so that the grown-ups could see it. They always need to have things explained. So my Drawing Number Two looked like this: This time, the grown-up's response was to advise me to lay aside my drawings of boa constrictors, whether from the inside or the outside, and devote myself to geography, history, arithmetic, and grammar.

That is why, at the age of six, I gave up what might have been a magnificent career as a painter. I had been disheartened by the failure of Drawing Number One and Number Two. Grown-ups never understand anything by themselves, and it is tiresome for children to be always and forever explaining things to them.

So, then I chose another profession and learned to pilot airplanes. I have flown a little over all parts of the world; geography has been advantageous to me. At a glance, I can distinguish China from Arizona. If one gets lost in the night, such knowledge is valuable.

In this life, I have had many encounters with many people who have been concerned with matters of consequence. I

Velocity Reading

have lived a great deal among grown-ups. I have seen them intimately, close at hand. And that hasn't much improved my opinion of them.

Whenever I met one of them who seemed to me at all clear-sighted, I tried the experiment of showing him my Drawing Number One, which I have always kept. I would try to find out if this person was adequately understood. But whoever it was, he, or she, would always say: "That is a hat." But, of course, I would never talk to that person about boa constrictors, ancient forests, or stars. Instead, I would bring myself down to his level. I would speak to him about the bridge, golf, politics, and neckties. And the grown-up would be exceptionally pleased to have met such a sensible man.

CHAPTER 2

So, I lived alone, without anyone I could talk to, until I had an accident with my plane in the Desert Sahara six years ago. Something broke in my engine. And as I had with me neither a mechanic nor any passengers, I set myself to attempt the complex repairs all alone. It was a question of life or death for me: I had scarcely enough drinking water to last a week.

I slept on the sand the first night, a thousand miles from any human habitation. I was more isolated than a shipwrecked sailor on a raft in the middle of the ocean. Thus, you can imagine my amazement at sunrise when an odd little voice awakened me. It said:
"If you please--draw me a sheep!"

"What!"
"Draw me a sheep!"
I jumped to my feet, completely dumbfounded. I blinked my eyes hard. I looked carefully all around me. And I saw a most extraordinary small person standing there examining me with great seriousness. So here you may see the best portrait that, later, I was able to make of him. But my drawing is indeed very much less charming than its model.

That, however, is not my fault. The grown-ups discouraged me in my painter's career when I was six years old, and I never learned to draw anything except boas from the outside and boas from the inside.

Now I stared at this sudden apparition with my eyes, somewhat starting my head in astonishment. Remember, I had crashed a thousand miles from any inhabited region in the desert. And yet my little man seemed neither to be straying uncertainly among the sands nor fainting from fatigue, hunger, thirst, or fear. On the contrary, nothing about him suggested a child lost in the middle of the desert, a thousand miles from any human habitation.

When at last I was able to speak, I said to him:
"But--what are you doing here?"
And in answer, he repeated, very slowly, as if he were speaking of a matter of great consequence:
"If you please--draw me a sheep . . ."
When a mystery is too overpowering, one dares not disobey. Absurd as it might seem, a thousand miles from any human habitation and in danger of death, I took a sheet of paper and my fountain pen out of my pocket. But

Velocity Reading

then I remembered how my studies had been concentrated on geography, history, arithmetic, and grammar, and I told the little chap (a little crossly, too) that I did not know how to draw. He answered me:
"That doesn't matter. Draw me a sheep . . ."

But I had never drawn a sheep. So, I drew for him one of the two pictures I had drawn so often. It was that of the boa constrictor from the outside. And I was astounded to hear the little fellow greet it with,
"No, no, no! I do not want an elephant inside a boa constrictor. A boa constrictor is very dangerous, and an elephant is very cumbersome. Where I live, everything is very small. What I need is a sheep. Draw me a sheep."

So, then I made a drawing.
He looked at it carefully, then he said:
"No. This sheep is already very sickly. Make me another."
So, I made another drawing.
My friend smiled gently and indulgently.
"You see yourself," he said, "that this is not a sheep. This is a ram. It has horns."

So, then I did my drawing over once more.
But it was rejected too, just like the others.
"This one is too old. I want a sheep that will live a long time."
By this time, my patience was exhausted because I was in a hurry to start taking my engine apart. So, I tossed off this drawing.

And I threw out an explanation with it.

"This is only his box. The sheep you asked for is inside."
I was astonished to see a light break over the face of my young judge:
"That is exactly the way I wanted it! Do you think this sheep will have to have a great deal of grass?"
"Why?" "Because where I live, everything is very small . . ."
"There will surely be enough grass for him," I said. "It is a very small sheep that I have given you."
He bent his head over the drawing.
"Not so small that--Look! He has gone to sleep . . ."
And that is how I made the acquaintance of the little prince.

CHAPTER 3

It took me a long time to learn where he came from. The little prince, who asked me many questions, never seemed to hear the ones I asked him. It was from words dropped by chance that, little by little, everything was revealed to me.
The first time he saw my airplane, for instance (I shall not draw my plane; that would be much too complicated for me), he asked me:
"What is that object?"
"That is not an object. It flies. It is an airplane. It is my airplane."
And I was proud to have him learn that I could fly.
He cried out, then:
"What! You dropped down from the sky?"
"Yes," I answered modestly.

Velocity Reading

"Oh! That is funny!" And the little prince broke into a lovely peal of laughter, which irritated me very much. I like my misfortunes to be taken seriously.

Then he added:
"So, you, too, come from the sky! Which is your planet?"
At that moment, I caught a gleam of light in the impenetrable mystery of his presence; and I demanded, abruptly:
"Do you come from another planet?"
But he did not reply. Instead, he tossed his head gently, without taking his eyes from my plane:
"It is true that on that you can't have come from very far away . . ."

And he sank into a reverie, which lasted a long time. Then, taking my sheep out of his pocket, he buried himself in the contemplation of his treasure.

You can imagine how this half-confidence aroused my curiosity about the "other planets." So, naturally, I made a great effort to learn more about this subject.

"My little man, where do you come from? What is this 'where I live,' of which you speak? Where do you want to take your sheep?"
After a reflective silence, he answered:
"The thing that is so good about the box you have given me is that he can use it at night as his house."
"That is so. And if you are good, I will give you a string, too, so that you can tie him during the day and a post to tie him to."

Normal Text

But the little prince seemed shocked by this offer:
"Tie him! What a queer idea!"
"But if you don't tie him," I said, "he will wander off somewhere and get lost."
My friend broke into another peal of laughter:
"But where do you think he would go?"
"Anywhere. Straight ahead of him."
Then the little prince said, earnestly:
"That doesn't matter. Where I live, everything is so small!"
And, with perhaps a hint of sadness, he added:
"Straight ahead of him, nobody can go very far . . ."

CHAPTER 4

I had thus learned a second fact of great importance: this was that the planet the little prince came from was scarcely any larger than a house!

But that did not surprise me much. I knew very well that in addition to the great planets--such as the Earth, Jupiter, Mars, and Venus--to which we have given names, there are also hundreds of others, some of which are so small that one has a hard time seeing them through the telescope. When an astronomer discovers one of these, he does not give it a name but only a number. He might call it, for example, "Asteroid 325."
I have serious reason to believe that the planet from which the little prince came is the asteroid known as B- 612. This asteroid has only once been seen through the telescope. That was by a Turkish astronomer in 1909.

Velocity Reading

On making his discovery, the astronomer presented it to the International Astronomical Congress in a great demonstration. But he was in Turkish costume, so nobody would believe what he said.
Grown-ups are like that . . .

Fortunately, however, for the reputation of Asteroid B-612, a Turkish dictator made a law that his subjects, under pain of death, should change to European costume. So, in 1920 the astronomer gave his demonstration all over again, dressed in impressive style and elegance. And this time, everybody accepted his report.

If I have told you these details about the asteroid and noted its number for you, it is because of the grown-ups and their ways. When you tell them that you have made a new friend, they never ask you any questions about essential matters. They never say to you, "What does his voice sound like? What games does he love best? Does he collect butterflies?" Instead, they demand: "How old is he? How many brothers has he? How much does he weigh? How much money does his father make?" Only from these figures do they think they have learned anything about him.

If you were to say to the grown-ups: "I saw a beautiful house made of rosy brick, with geraniums in the windows and doves on the roof," they would not be able to get an idea of that house at all. You would have to tell them: "I saw a house that cost $20,000." Then they would exclaim: "Oh, what a pretty house that is!"

Just so, you might say to them: "The proof that the little prince existed is that he was charming, that he laughed, and that he was looking for a sheep. If anybody wants a sheep, that is proof that he exists." And what good would it do to tell them that? They would shrug their shoulders and treat you like a child. But if you said to them: "The planet he came from is Asteroid B-612," they would be convinced and leave you in peace with their questions.

They are like that. One must not hold it against them. Children should always show great forbearance toward grown-up people.

But certainly, for us who understand life, figures are a matter of indifference. I should have liked to begin this story in the fashion of the fairy tales. I should have like to say: "Once upon a time, and there was a little prince who lived on a planet that was scarcely any bigger than himself, and who needed a sheep . . ."

That would have given my story a much greater air of truth to those who understand life.

For I do not want anyone to read my book carelessly. I have suffered too much grief in setting down these memories. Six years have already passed since my friend went away from me with his sheep. If I try to describe him here, it is to make sure that I shall not forget him. To forget a friend is sad. Not everyone has had a friend. And if I ignore him, I may become like the grown-ups who are no longer interested in anything but figures . . .

Velocity Reading

It is for that purpose, again, that I have bought a box of paints and some pencils. It is hard to take up drawing again at my age when I have never made any pictures except those of the boa constrictor from the outside and the boa constrictor from the inside since I was six. I shall try to make my portraits as true to life as possible. But I am not at all sure of success. One drawing goes along all right, and another has no resemblance to its subject. I make some errors, too, in the little prince's height: in one place, he is too tall, and in another, too short. And I feel some doubts about the color of his costume. So, I fumble along as best I can, now good and evil, and I generally hope to be fair-to-middling.

In specific, more important details, I shall make mistakes, also. But that is something that will not be my fault. My friend never explained anything to me. He thought, perhaps, that I was like himself. But I, alas, do not know how to see sheep through the walls of boxes. Maybe I am a little like the grown-ups. I have had to grow old.

End of text

To do
Repeat the exercise.
You can, of course, practice with your texts now.

This technique is the basis for *Velocity Reading*.
It is crucial to practice and do it right.
Please do it again.

Take your time to do it right, slowly at first, and feel comfortable.

Let your brain lead. If your brain wants to know more it will accelerate the rhythm, and your eyes will follow ...

Otherwise, forcing your eyes, you press the pace, and your will to go fast will take over. It is not the best technique. You will succeed in moving faster but at the expense of understanding and memory.

The best motivation is to want to know what happens next. i.e., be driven by your brain, mind, and interest to learn more.

It increases your interest, judgment, concentration, and text memory.

The Objective Was
To practice on a standard text.

What You Learned
- You get your eyes to *reading fewer glances per line* with standard text.
- You have used your eyes to read from the *second or third word at the beginning of the line*.
- You have increased your comfort in using this technique on a standard text.

Explanations
The exercise on a standard text may have slightly disoriented you. It's normal. There were no more

Velocity Reading

"crutches" to help you: the text is no longer in columns and no longer repeats itself.

Note
You should have noticed that:
- It was a bit more difficult at first.
- However, you now tend to look for the keywords when you try to read in a few glances.
- Sometimes it takes you four glances but also that on other lines, two glances only. Maybe even one on the lines where the character speaks.
- You may have noticed that sometimes you could "guess" in advance the following words. It is because you have already read it and are more focused. You will see the same phenomenon in a text you have never read.

Evaluate yourself

It's time to take stock.
How you read should have changed a lot already.

Here is a little assessment you can do.
Read the standard text of the lesson 3 once more, with a timer.

Please do that test *at a speed you feel **comfortable*** with.

Please don't try to prove to yourself how fast you can read. **Do not** try to read as fast as possible.

This is a mistake. It is not a demonstration or a contest. If you push too hard, the result might make you proud, but it will not be what you can do in an everyday context and for a long reading session.

It will give you the illusion you can achieve such performance and mislead you in your progress. Also, it will disappoint you when you do not readily reproduce that result.
So, do the exercise a**t a comfortable pace** to measure your **average performance** and know where you stand.

If you take 12 minutes or more, you still are a slow reader. But in under 6 minutes, you are already a fast reader.

Velocity Reading

Where you stand & the next steps

- You know you can read several words at once.
- You can generally read each line in 2 or 3 glances only.
- By reading the keywords, you understand the sentence's meaning without having to read all the words and the articles.
- Your brain manages to do this naturally.
- You read faster.
- You are more focused.
- You tend to want to skip uninteresting parts and guess what is written without losing much of the text.
  And this is just the beginning.
  Are you excited to continue? I certainly hope so!

Recommendation
Reading in two or three glances per line
is the basis for reading faster without having to skip any text.

Since this technique is the most important basic one
you will always be able to rely on it.
It allows you to read faster, at a pace that helps your brain to stay focused.
You can do that on any text, even important ones, because you are not skipping or missing anything.

Practice often if it is not already a usual way to read for you now.
Suggestion: Always let your brain dictate the rhythm.
Why?
- You read to understand, learn or relax.
- Not to win speed competitions.

Evaluate Yourself

- It will be easier.
- It will be less tiring.
-

Later, you will learn ways to discipline the brain under certain circumstances. But it must be your thoughts that lead.

Results
Are you pleased with your results so far?
Was it easy to learn and practice?
Will you ever read otherwise from now on?
If you improve your basic reading skills,
do you realize the number of hours
you will be **saving** in the future
or
how much **more** knowledge will you be
able to acquire much **faster**?

Also, your retention must have increased because your attention has increased.

Is your brain driving, hungry for more?
Speed is a tool. It is not the objective.
But adequately trained, it will increase significantly.
Considering all the additional time or information
you will be able to acquire, do you think it will be worth
many times, your investment in *Velocity Reading* so far?
We hope you do.

Next

You have completed Part One.

Velocity Reading

Because of its importance, learning to have a wider span was the only lesson for the whole section.

There are two more Parts.
Next, Part Two is all the other tools and techniques to scan, skim, and search a document or book.

And Part Three is about the main tactic when having to read a new book. Of course, it will require the tools of section two to be at your best to exploit that tactic fully. But, if you wish, you can go right to Part Three to make a quantum leap and learn how to approach a new book like a pro. But don't forget to return two Part Two to acquire the additional techniques that will help you do it even faster.

PART TWO
TOOLS

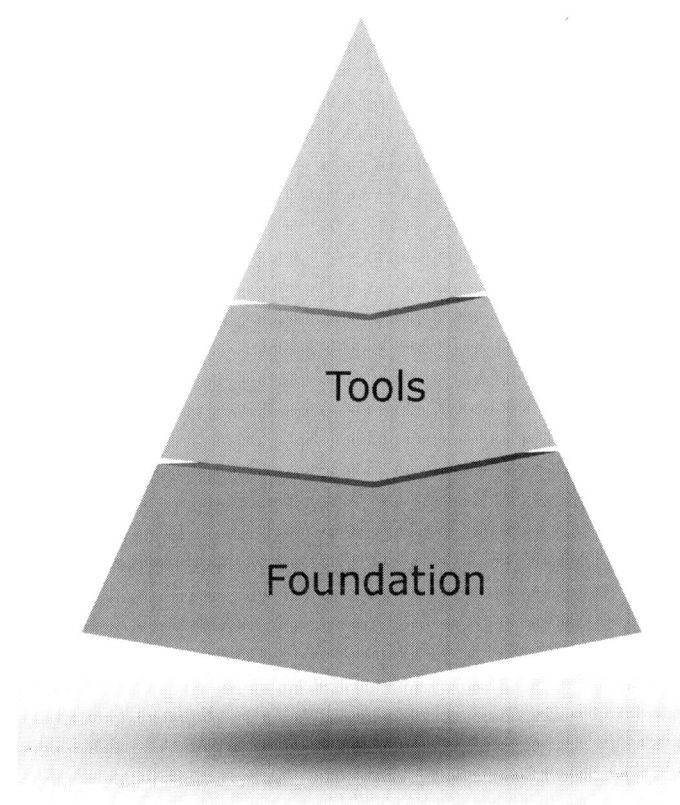

More tools to read better & faster

Velocity Reading

*V*elocityReading. Lesson 4. **Vertical Reading Techniques**

"When one cannot read, one has eyes without seeing."

Maxime of ancient Greece.

LESSON 4. VERTICAL READING TECHNIQUES.
YOUR EYES AND YOUR VISION ARE CIRCULAR

This lesson will help you to:
1) Enlarge your vertical vision span.
2) Read on mobile devices.

The objective
Enlarge your vertical vision span.

A little reminder...
Your eyes and your vision are circular. In other words, you see both vertically and horizontally. When we read, we forget because the texts are written horizontally.
So, it's a habit.
Proof: you can see a column of figures in Excel without difficulty or "Books" in the image on the previous page.

Instruction
Read the following text by trying to see all the text between two lines at a glance.
Again, please go slowly. Do not try to go too fast. Let your brain and your eye gain experience. Get used to it.

Velocity Reading

Beginning of the text

TO LEON WERTH

I ask the indulgence
of the children
who may read

---

this book for
dedicating it to a grown-up.

I have a serious reason:
he is the best friend I have
in the world.

I have another reason:
this grown-up understands

---

everything, even
books about children.

I have a third reason:
he lives in France where
he is hungry and cold.

Vertical Reading

He needs cheering up.
If all these reasons
are not enough,
I will dedicate
the book to the child from
whom

———————————

this grown-up grew.
All grown-ups were once
children

———————————

although few of them
remember it.

———————————

And so, I correct my
dedication: TO

———————————

LEON WERTH
WHEN HE WAS
A LITTLE BOY.

———————————

CHAPTER I
Once
when I was six years old

———————————

I saw a
magnificent picture

Velocity Reading

in a book,

_____

called True Stories from
Nature,
about the primeval forest.
It was a picture
of a boa constrictor
in the act

_____

of swallowing
an animal.

_____

Here is a copy of the drawing.
In the book, it said:

_____

"Boa constrictors swallow
their prey whole,
without chewing it.

_____

After that
they are not
able to move,

_____

and
they sleep
through the
six months

Vertical Reading

that they need
for digestion."

I pondered deeply, then, over
the adventures
of the jungle.

And after
some work with
a colored pencil

I succeeded
in making
my first drawing.

My Drawing Number One. It
looked something like this:

I showed my masterpiece to
the grown-ups,

and asked them whether
the drawing frightened them.

But they answered: "Frighten?
Why should anyone be
frightened by

Velocity Reading

a hat?"

My drawing
was not
a picture of
a hat.
It was a picture
of a
boa constrictor digesting
an elephant.

But since
the grown-ups
were not able to understand
it,

I made another drawing:

I drew
the inside of
a boa constrictor,

---

so that the
grown-ups
could see it.

They always need to have
things explained.

Vertical Reading

My Drawing Number Two
looked like this:

The grown-ups' response,
this time,

was to advise me
to lay aside
my drawings of
boa constrictors,

whether from the inside or
the outside,

and devote myself instead to
geography,
history,
arithmetic,
and grammar.

That is why,
at the age of six,
I gave up

what might have been a
magnificent career as a

Velocity Reading

painter.

I had been disheartened
by the failure
of my
Drawing Number One and my
Drawing Number Two.

Grown-ups
never understand
anything by themselves,
and it is
tiresome
for children
to be always
and forever
explaining things to them.

So, then
I chose
another profession,

---

and learned
to pilot
airplanes.

I have flown a little over
all parts of the world;

Vertical Reading

and it is true
that geography
has been very
useful to me.

At a glance
I can distinguish
China from Arizona.

If one gets lost
in the night,
such knowledge
is valuable.

In the course
of this life
I have had
a great many
encounters
with
a great many
people

who have been concerned
with matters of consequence.

I have lived

Velocity Reading

a great deal
among
grown-ups.

I have
seen them
intimately,
close at hand.

_____

And that hasn't
much improved
my opinion of them.

_____

Whenever
I met one
of them

who seemed to me
at all clear-sighted,
I tried the experiment of
showing him
my Drawing Number One,

_____

which I have
always kept.

Vertical Reading

I would try
to find out, so,

_____

if this was a person
of true understanding.

_____

But whoever it was, he, or
she,
would always say:
"That is a hat."

Then
I would never
talk
to that person
about
boa constrictors,

_____

or primeval forests,
or stars.

I would
bring myself down
to his level.

I would talk to him about
bridge,
and golf,
and politics,
and neckties.

Velocity Reading

And the grown-up would be
greatly pleased

to have met
such a
sensible man.

CHAPTER II

So I lived my life
alone,
without anyone

that I could
talk to,
until

I had an accident with my
plane
in the Desert
of Sahara,
six years ago.

Something
was broken

Vertical Reading

in my engine.

And as
I had with me
neither
a mechanic
nor
any passengers,

I set myself
to attempt
the difficult repairs
all alone.
It was
a question
of life
or
death
for me:

I had
scarcely enough drinking
water
to last a week.

The first night,
then,
I went to sleep
on the sand,

Velocity Reading

a thousand miles
from any
human habitation.

I was
more isolated
than a
shipwrecked sailor

on a raft
in the middle
of the ocean.

Thus
you can imagine
my amazement,
at sunrise,

when I was
awakened
by an odd
little voice.

It said:
"If you please...
draw me a sheep!"

Vertical Reading

"What!"
"Draw me a sheep!"

I jumped
to my feet,
completely
thunderstruck.

I blinked
my eyes
hard.

I looked
carefully
all around me.

And I saw
a most extraordinary small
person,

---

who stood
there
examining me
with great
seriousness.

Here
you may see

Velocity Reading

the best portrait
that, later,
I was able
to make
of him.

But
my drawing
is certainly
very much
less charming
than its model.

That,
however,
is not
my fault.

The
grown-ups discouraged me
in my
painter's career

---

when I was
six years old,

---

and
I never learned
to draw

Vertical Reading

anything,

---

except
boas
from
the outside
and
boas from the inside.
Now
I started
at this
sudden apparition
with
my eyes

---

fairly
starting
out of
my head
in astonishment.

Remember,
I had
crashed
in the desert
a thousand

---

miles
from

Velocity Reading

any
inhabited
region.

And yet
my little man
seemed
neither
to be

straying
uncertainly
among
the
sands,

---

nor
to be
fainting
from
fatigue

or

hunger
or
thirst
or
fear.

Vertical Reading

Nothing
about him
gave any
suggestion of
a child lost

in the middle
of the desert,
a thousand miles
from any
human habitation.

When at last
I was able
to speak,
I said to him:

"But...
what
are you
doing here?"

And
in answer
he repeated,
very slowly,

Velocity Reading

as if
he was
speaking
of a matter
of great
consequence:

"If you please...
draw me a sheep . . ."

When
a mystery
is too overpowering. One dare
not disobey.

Absurd
as it might seem
to me,

---

a thousand miles
from any human habitation

---

and
in danger
of death,

Vertical Reading

I took out
of my
pocket
a sheet
of
paper
and
my
fountain-pen.

But then
I remembered
how my studies
had been

---

concentrated on
geography,
history,
arithmetic
and grammar,
and I told
the little chap
(a little crossly, too) that I did
not know how to draw.

He answered me: "That
doesn't matter. Draw me a
sheep . . ."

Velocity Reading

But
I had never
drawn a sheep.

So, I drew
for him
one of the two
pictures
I had drawn
so often.

It was
that of
the boa constrictor from the
outside.

And
I was astounded
to hear
the little fellow
greet it with,

"No, no, no!
I do not want
an elephant
inside
a boa constrictor.
A boa constrictor
is a very dangerous creature,

Vertical Reading

and
an elephant
is
very cumbersome.

Where I live,
everything
is very small.

What I need
is a sheep.
Draw me a sheep."

So,
then I made
a drawing.

He looked at it carefully,
then he said:

"No.
This sheep
is already
very sickly.

Velocity Reading

Make me another."

So
I made
another
drawing.

My
friend
smiled
gently
and
indulgently.

"You see yourself,"
he said,
"that this is not a sheep.
This is a ram.
It has horns."

So
then I did
my drawing
over
once more.

But it was rejected too,

just like the others.

"This one is too old.
I want a sheep
that will live
a long time."

By this time
my patience
was exhausted,

because
I was in a hurry
to start
taking
my engine
apart.

So, I tossed off
this drawing.
And I threw out an
explanation with it.

"This is only his box. The
sheep you asked for is inside."

I was astonished
to see a light break
over the face of
my young judge:

Velocity Reading

"That is exactly
the way
I wanted it!

Do you think
that this sheep
will have to
have a great deal
of grass?"

———————

"Why?"
"Because
where I live
everything is very small . . ."

"There will surely
be enough grass
for him,"
I said.

"It is
a very small sheep
that I have given you."

———————

He bent his head over the
drawing.
"Not so small that...

Look!

Vertical Reading

He has gone to sleep . . ."

And that is how I made the acquaintance of the little prince.

End of text

You can do the exercise several times.
As much as possible, no more than 3-5 minutes at a time.

The Objective Was
Enlarge your vertical vision span.

What You Learned
- You accustomed your eyes to reading *vertically*.
- You have used your eyes to *see several words on several lines*.
- You have learned to read several lines in a single look.

Explanations
You see both vertically and horizontally.
When we read, we forget that we see also vertically because the texts are written horizontally.
So, it's a habit.
You have seen it yourself: you can read several lines at once.

Velocity Reading

Note
You should have noticed that:

- It is easy.
- Reading two or three lines at a glance is easy when there are not too many words on a line.
- If you have observed well, in some cases, there were 5, 6, or even up to 11 words to read between two lines.
- You probably managed to easily see up to 7 lines of words in one glance". If not, you will see that by practicing a little, it will become possible.

In addition,

- You will realize that you now see the words on the following line in a text written normally like this one. In many accessible texts, you will know in advance or see the words on two or three lines simultaneously.
- For your information, trying to see/read 3 or 5 lines at a time is the easiest to practice, compared to even numbers like 2, 4, 6...
- Three lines at a time are the most beneficial to master.
- More is possible and will be helpful in future exercises and specific contexts. You will get more explanations when you reach those exercises.

Recommendation
Practice this exercise. It increases your flexibility to "read" and see wider vertically.

You will find it very useful when you search in a document.

Vertical Reading

With practice, you will see broader and higher simultaneously if you read a lot.

With practice, you can read five lines at a time in some documents and see the full text.

But capturing three lines at once is what you will be able to do the most effortlessly and is quite remarkable, wouldn't you agree?

Just put that back in perspective. When you started reading Velocity Reading, maybe you were reading almost one word at a time.

In addition, you might have been worried about less comprehension if you read faster or did not read everything.

What do you think now?

So, may we suggest to be reasonable. Although you know what you can do, make sure what you do keeps you in control, comfortable, and focused on learning and understanding first, speed second.

Velocity Reading

*V*elocityReading. Lesson 5. Vertical Reading Techniques.

"If you know how to read, then the whole world opens up to you."

Barack Obama

LESSON 5. VERTICAL READING TECHNIQUES 2.
READ SEVERAL WORDS ON SEVERAL LINES ON SEVERAL COLUMNS

The objective
Increase your flexibility.
Instruction
- Read this text by trying to see all the text between the lines at a glance.
- Read from left to right.
This is as in Lesson 2.1. The same text is repeated three times.

Again, please go slowly.
Do not try to go too fast at first.
Let your brain and your eye gain experience. Get used to it.

Velocity Reading

Beginning of the text

TO LEON WERTH	TO LEON WERTH	TO LEON WERTH
I ask the indulgence of the children who may read	I ask the indulgence of the children who may read	I ask the indulgence of the children who may read
this book for dedicating it to a grown-up.	this book for dedicating it to a grown-up.	this book for dedicating it to a grown-up.
I have a serious reason: he is the best friend I have in the world.	I have a serious reason: he is the best friend I have in the world.	I have a serious reason: he is the best friend I have in the world.
I have another rea son: this grown-up understands	I have another reas on: this grown-up understands	I have another reaso n: this grown-up understands

Vertical Reading

everything, even books about children.	everything, even books about children.	everything, even books about children.
I have a third reason: he lives in France where he is hungry and cold.	I have a third reason: he lives in France where he is hungry and cold.	I have a third reason: he lives in France where he is hungry and cold.
He needs heering up. If all these reasons are not enough,	He needs heering up. If all these reasons are not enough,	He needs cheering up. If all these reasons are not enough,
I will dedicate the book to the child from whom	I will dedicate the book to the child from whom	I will dedicate the book to the child from whom
this grown up grew. All grown-ups were once children	this grown-up grew. All grown-ups were once children	this grown-up grew. All grown-ups were once children

Velocity Reading

| although few of them remember it. | although few of them remember it. | although few of them remember it. |

And so, I correct my dedication: TO

And so, I correct my dedication: TO

And so, I correct my dedication: TO

LEON WERTH
WHEN HE
WAS
A LITTLE BOY

LEON WERTH
WHEN HE
WAS
A LITTLE BOY

LEON WERTH
WHEN HE
WAS
A LITTLE BOY

CHAPTER I

CHAPTER I

CHAPTER I

Once
when I was six
years old

Once
when I was six
years old

Once
when I was six
years old

I saw a
magnificent
picture
in a book,

I saw a
magnificent
picture
in a book,

I saw a
magnificent
picture
in a book,

called True
Stories from
Nature,

called True
Stories from
Nature,

called True Stories
from
Nature,

Vertical Reading

about the
primeval forest.

It was a picture
of a
boa constrictor
in the act

of swallowing
an animal.

Here is a copy of
the drawing.
In the book, it
said:

"Boa constrictors
swallow
their prey whole,
without chewing
it.

After that
they are not
able to move,

---

about the
primeval forest.

It was a picture
of a
boa constrictor
in the act

of swallowing
an animal.

Here is a copy of
the drawing.
In the book, it
said:

"Boa constrictors
swallow
their prey whole,
without chewing
it.

After that
they are not
able to move,

---

about the
primeval forest.

It was a picture
of a
boa constrictor
in the act

of swallowing
an animal.

Here is a copy of
the drawing.
In the book, it
said:

"Boa constrictors
swallow
their prey whole,
without chewing
it.

After that
they are not
able to move,

Velocity Reading

and they sleep through the six months	and they sleep through the six months	and they sleep through the six months
that they need for digestion."	that they need for digestion."	that they need for digestion."
I pondered deeply, then, over the adventures of the jungle.	I pondered deeply, then, over the adventures of the jungle.	I pondered deeply, then, over the adventures of the jungle.
And after some work with a colored pencil	And after some work with a colored pencil	And after some work with a colored pencil
I succeeded in making my first drawing.	I succeeded in making my first drawing.	I succeeded in making my first drawing.
My Drawing Number One. It looked something like this:	My Drawing Number One. It looked something like this:	My Drawing Number One. It looked something like this:

Vertical Reading

I showed my masterpiece to the grown-ups,	I showed my masterpiece to the grown-ups,	I showed my masterpiece to the grown-ups,
and asked them whether the drawing frightened them.	and asked them whether the drawing frightened them.	and asked them whether the drawing frightened them.
But they answered: "Frighten? Why should anyone be frightened by a hat?"	But they answered: "Frighten? Why should anyone be frightened by a hat?"	But they answered: "Frighten? Why should anyone be frightened by a hat?"
My drawing was not a picture of a hat.	My drawing was not a picture of a hat.	My drawing was not a picture of a hat.
It was a picture of a boa constrictor digesting an elephant.	It was a picture of a boa constrictor digesting an elephant.	It was a picture of a boa constrictor digesting an elephant.

Velocity Reading

But since the grown-ups were not able to understand it,	But since the grown-ups were not able to understand it,	But since the grown-ups were not able to understand it,
I made another drawing:	I made another drawing:	I made another drawing:
I drew the inside of a boa constrictor,	I drew the inside of a boa constrictor,	I drew the inside of a boa constrictor,
so that the grown-ups could see it.	so that the grown-ups could see it.	so that the grown-ups could see it.
They always need to have things explained.	They always need to have things explained.	They always need to have things explained.
My Drawing Number Two looked like this:	My Drawing Number Two looked like this:	My Drawing Number Two looked like this:

Vertical Reading

The grown-ups'
response,
this time,

was to advise me
to lay aside
my drawings of
boa constrictors,

whether from the
inside or
the outside,

and devote
myself instead to
geography,
history,
arithmetic,
and grammar.

That is why,
at the age of six,
I gave up

what might have
been a

Velocity Reading

magnificent career as a painter.	magnificent career as a painter.	magnificent career as a painter.
I had been disheartened by the failure of my Drawing Number One and my Drawing Number Two.	I had been disheartened by the failure of my Drawing Number One and my Drawing Number Two.	I had been disheartened by the failure of my Drawing Number One and my Drawing Number Two.
Grown-ups never understand anything by themselves,	Grown-ups never understand anything by themselves,	Grown-ups never understand anything by themselves,
and it is tiresome for children to be always and forever explaining things to them.	and it is tiresome for children to be always and forever explaining things to them.	and it is tiresome for children to be always and forever explaining things to them.

Vertical Reading

So, then
I chose
another
profession,

and learned
to pilot
airplanes.

I have flown a
little over
all parts of the
world;

and it is true
that geography
has been very
useful to me.

At a glance
I can distinguish
China from
Arizona.

If one gets lost
in the night,
such knowledge
is valuable.

So, then
I chose
another
profession,

and learned
to pilot
airplanes.

I have flown a
little over
all parts of the
world;

and it is true
that geography
has been very
useful to me.

At a glance
I can distinguish
China from
Arizona.

If one gets lost
in the night,
such knowledge
is valuable.

So, then
I chose
another
profession,

and learned
to pilot
airplanes.

I have flown a
little over
all parts of the
world;

and it is true
that geography
has been very
useful to me.

At a glance
I can distinguish
China from
Arizona.

If one gets lost
in the night,
such knowledge
is valuable.

Velocity Reading

In the course
of this life
I have had
a great many
encounters

with
a great many
people

who have been
concerned
with matters of
consequence.

I have lived
a great deal
among
grown-ups.

I have
seen them
intimately,

close at hand.
And that hasn't

In the course
of this life
I have had
a great many
encounters

with
a great many
people

who have been
concerned
with matters of
consequence.

I have lived
a great deal
among
grown-ups.

I have
seen them
intimately,

close at hand.
And that hasn't

In the course
of this life
I have had
a great many
encounters

with
a great many
people

who have been
concerned
with matters of
consequence.

I have lived
a great deal
among
grown-ups.

I have
seen them
intimately,

close at hand.
And that hasn't

Vertical Reading

much improved my opinion of them.	much improved my opinion of them.	much improved my opinion of them.
Whenever I met one of them	Whenever I met one of them	Whenever I met one of them
who seemed to me at all clear-sighted,	who seemed to me at all clear-sighted,	who seemed to me at all clear-sighted,
I tried the experiment of showing him my Drawing Number One,	I tried the experiment of showing him my Drawing Number One,	I tried the experiment of showing him my Drawing Number One,
which I have always kept. I would try to find out, so,	which I have always kept. I would try to find out, so,	which I have always kept. I would try to find out, so,
if this was a person of true understanding.	if this was a person of true understanding.	if this was a person of true understanding.

Velocity Reading

But whoever it
was, he, or
she,
would always
say:
"That is a hat."

Then
I would never
talk
to that person
about
boa constrictors,

or primeval
forests,
or stars.

I would
bring myself
down
to his level.

I would talk to
him about
bridge,
and golf,
and politics,
and neckties.

But whoever it
was, he, or
she,
would always
say:
"That is a hat."

Then
I would never
talk
to that person
about
boa constrictors,

or primeval
forests,
or stars.

I would
bring myself
down
to his level.

I would talk to
him about
bridge,
and golf,
and politics,
and neckties.

But whoever it
was, he, or
she,
would always
say:
"That is a hat."

Then
I would never
talk
to that person
about
boa constrictors,

or primeval
forests,
or stars.

I would
bring myself
down
to his level.

I would talk to
him about
bridge,
and golf,
and politics,
and neckties.

Vertical Reading

And the grown-
up would be
greatly pleased

to have met
such a
sensible man.

CHAPTER II

So I lived my
life
alone,
without anyone

that I could
talk to,
until

I had an accident
with my
plane
in the Desert
of Sahara,
six years ago.

And the grown-
up would be
greatly pleased

to have met
such a
sensible man.

CHAPTER II

So I lived my
life
alone,
without anyone

that I could
talk to,
until

I had an accident
with my
plane
in the Desert
of Sahara,
six years ago.

And the grown-up
would be
greatly pleased

to have met
such a
sensible man.

CHAPTER II

So I lived my
life
alone,
without anyone

that I could
talk to,
until

I had an accident
with my
plane
in the Desert
of Sahara,
six years ago.

Velocity Reading

Something
was broken
in my engine.

Something
was broken
in my engine.

Something
was broken
in my engine.

And as
I had with me
neither
a mechanic
nor
any passengers,

And as
I had with me
neither
a mechanic
nor
any passengers,

And as
I had with me
neither
a mechanic
nor
any passengers,

I set myself
to attempt
the difficult
repairs
all alone.

I set myself
to attempt
the difficult
repairs
all alone.

I set myself
to attempt
the difficult
repairs
all alone.

It was
a question
of life
or
death
for me:

It was
a question
of life
or
death
for me:

It was
a question
of life
or
death
for me:

I had
scarcely enough
drinking
water
to last a week.

I had
scarcely enough
drinking
water
to last a week.

I had
scarcely enough
drinking
water
to last a week.

Vertical Reading

The first night,
then,
I went to sleep
on the sand,

a thousand
miles
from any
human
habitation.

I was
more isolated
than a
shipwrecked
sailor

on a raft
in the middle
of the ocean.

Thus
you can imagine
my amazement,
at sunrise,

Velocity Reading

when I was
awakened
by an odd
little voice.

It said:
"If you please...
draw me a
sheep!"

"What!"
"Draw me a
sheep!"

I jumped
to my feet,
completely
thunderstruck.

I blinked
my eyes
hard.

I looked
carefully
all around me.

when I was
awakened
by an odd
little voice.

It said:
"If you please...
draw me a
sheep!"

"What!"
"Draw me a
sheep!"

I jumped
to my feet,
completely
thunderstruck.

I blinked
my eyes
hard.

I looked
carefully
all around me.

when I was
awakened
by an odd
little voice.

It said:
"If you please...
draw me a
sheep!"

"What!"
"Draw me a
sheep!"

I jumped
to my feet,
completely
thunderstruck.

I blinked
my eyes
hard.

I looked
carefully
all around me.

Vertical Reading

And I saw
a most
extraordinary
small
person,

who stood
there
examining me
with great
seriousness.

Here
you may see
the best portrait
that, later,
I was able
to make
of him.

But
my drawing
is certainly
very much
less charming
than its model.

And I saw
a most
extraordinary
small
person,

who stood
there
examining me
with great
seriousness.

Here
you may see
the best portrait
that, later,
I was able
to make
of him.

But
my drawing
is certainly
very much
less charming
than its model.

And I saw
a most
extraordinary
small
person,

who stood
there
examining me
with great
seriousness.

Here
you may see
the best portrait
that, later,
I was able
to make
of him.

But
my drawing
is certainly
very much
less charming
than its model.

Velocity Reading

That, however, is not my fault.	That, however, is not my fault.	That, however, is not my fault.
The grown-ups discouraged me in my painter's career	The grown-ups discouraged me in my painter's career	The grown-ups discouraged me in my painter's career
when I was six years old,	when I was six years old,	when I was six years old,
and I never learned to draw anything,	and I never learned to draw anything,	and I never learned to draw anything,
except boas from the outside and boas from the inside.	except boas from the outside and boas from the inside.	except boas from the outside and boas from the inside.

Vertical Reading

Now
I stared
at this
sudden
apparition
with
my eyes

fairly
starting
out of
my head
in astonishment.

Remember,
I had
crashed
in the desert
a thousand
miles
from
any
inhabited
region.

And yet
my little man
seemed

Velocity Reading

neither to be	neither to be	neither to be
straying uncertainly among the sands,	straying uncertainly among the sands,	straying uncertainly among the sands,
nor to be fainting from fatigue or hunger or thirst or fear.	nor to be fainting from fatigue or hunger or thirst or fear.	nor to be fainting from fatigue or hunger or thirst or fear.
Nothing about him gave any suggestion of a child lost	Nothing about him gave any suggestion of a child lost	Nothing about him gave any suggestion of a child lost
in the middle of the desert,	in the middle of the desert,	in the middle of the desert,

Vertical Reading

a thousand miles
from any
human
habitation.

When at last
I was able
to speak,
I said to him:

"But...
what
are you
doing here?"

And
in answer
he repeated,
very slowly,

---

as if
he was
speaking
of a matter
of great
consequence:
"If you please...
draw me a sheep
. . ."

a thousand miles
from any
human
habitation.

When at last
I was able
to speak,
I said to him:

"But...
what
are you
doing here?"

And
in answer
he repeated,
very slowly,

---

as if
he was
speaking
of a matter
of great
consequence:
"If you please...
draw me a sheep
. . ."

a thousand miles
from any
human
habitation.

When at last
I was able
to speak,
I said to him:

"But...
what
are you
doing here?"

And
in answer
he repeated,
very slowly,

---

as if
he was
speaking
of a matter
of great
consequence:
"If you please...
draw me a sheep .
. ."

Velocity Reading

When a mystery is too overpowering. One dare not disobey.	When a mystery is too overpowering. One dare not disobey.	When a mystery is too overpowering. One dare not disobey.
Absurd as it might seem to me,	Absurd as it might seem to me,	Absurd as it might seem to me,
a thousand miles from any human habitation	a thousand miles from any human habitation	a thousand miles from any human habitation
and in danger of death,	and in danger of death,	and in danger of death,
I took out of my pocket a sheet of paper and	I took out of my pocket a sheet of paper and	I took out of my pocket a sheet of paper and

Vertical Reading

my
fountain-pen.

But then
I remembered
how my studies
had been

concentrated on
geography,
history,
arithmetic
and grammar,

and I told
the little chap
(a little crossly,
too) that I did
not know how to
draw.

He answered me:
"That
doesn't matter.
Draw me a
sheep . . ."

Velocity Reading

But
I had never
drawn a sheep.

So, I drew
for him
one of the two
pictures
I had drawn
so often.

It was
that of
the boa
constrictor from
the
outside.

And
I was astounded
to hear
the little fellow
greet it with,

"No, no, no!
I do not want
an elephant
inside
a boa constrictor.

But
I had never
drawn a sheep.

So, I drew
for him
one of the two
pictures
I had drawn
so often.

It was
that of
the boa
constrictor from
the
outside.

And
I was astounded
to hear
the little fellow
greet it with,

"No, no, no!
I do not want
an elephant
inside
a boa constrictor.

But
I had never
drawn a sheep.

So, I drew
for him
one of the two
pictures
I had drawn
so often.

It was
that of
the boa
constrictor from
the
outside.

And
I was astounded
to hear
the little fellow
greet it with,

"No, no, no!
I do not want
an elephant
inside
a boa constrictor.

Vertical Reading

A boa constrictor is a very dangerous creature,	A boa constrictor is a very dangerous creature,	A boa constrictor is a very dangerous creature,
and an elephant is very cumbersome.	and an elephant is very cumbersome.	and an elephant is very cumbersome.
Where I live, everything is very small.	Where I live, everything is very small.	Where I live, everything is very small.
What I need is a sheep. Draw me a sheep."	What I need is a sheep. Draw me a sheep."	What I need is a sheep. Draw me a sheep."
So, then I made a drawing.	So, then I made a drawing.	So, then I made a drawing.
He looked at it carefully, then he said:	He looked at it carefully, then he said:	He looked at it carefully, then he said:

Velocity Reading

"No.
This sheep
is already
very sickly.
Make me
another."

So
I made
another
drawing.

My
friend
smiled
gently
and
indulgently.

"You see
yourself,"
he said,
"that this is not a
sheep.
This is a ram.
It has horns."

Vertical Reading

So
then I did
my drawing
over
once more.

But it was
rejected too,
just like the
others.

"This one is too
old.
I want a sheep
that will live
a long time."

By this time
my patience
was exhausted,

because
I was in a hurry
to start
taking
my engine
apart.

So
then I did
my drawing
over
once more.

But it was
rejected too,
just like the
others.

"This one is too
old.
I want a sheep
that will live
a long time."

By this time
my patience
was exhausted,

because
I was in a hurry
to start
taking
my engine
apart.

So
then I did
my drawing
over
once more.

But it was rejected
too,
just like the
others.

"This one is too
old.
I want a sheep
that will live
a long time."

By this time
my patience
was exhausted,

because
I was in a hurry
to start
taking
my engine
apart.

Velocity Reading

So, I tossed off
this drawing.
And I threw out
an
explanation with
it.

"This is only his
box. The
sheep you asked
for is inside."

I was astonished
to see a light
break
over the face of
my young judge:

"That is exactly
the way
I wanted it!

Do you think
that this sheep
will have to
have a great deal
of grass?"

So, I tossed off
this drawing.
And I threw out
an
explanation with
it.

"This is only his
box. The
sheep, you asked
for is inside."

I was astonished
to see a light
break
over the face of
my young judge:

"That is exactly
the way
I wanted it!

Do you think
that this sheep
will have to
have a great deal
of grass?"

So, I tossed off
this drawing.
And I threw out
an
explanation with
it.

"This is only his
box. The
sheep you asked
for is inside."

I was astonished
to see a light
break
over the face of
my young judge:

"That is exactly
the way
I wanted it!

Do you think
that this sheep
will have to
have a great deal
of grass?"

Vertical Reading

"Why?"
"Because
where I live
everything is
tiny..."

"There will
surely
be enough grass
for him,"
I said.

"It is
a very small
sheep
that I have given
you."

He bent his head
over the
drawing.
"Not so small
that...

Look!
He has gone to
sleep..."

"Why?"
"Because
where I live
everything is
tiny..."

"There will
surely
be enough grass
for him,"
I said.

"It is
a very small
sheep
that I have given
you."

He bent his head
over the
drawing.
"Not so small
that...

Look!
He has gone to
sleep..."

"Why?"
"Because
where I live
everything is tiny.
.."

"There will
surely
be enough grass
for him,"
I said.

"It is
a very small
sheep
that I have given
you."

He bent his head
over the
drawing.
"Not so small
that...

Look!
He has gone to
sleep..."

Velocity Reading

And that is how I made the acquaintance of the little prince.	And that is how I made the acquaintance of the little prince.	And that is how I made the acquaintance of the little prince.

End of text

You can do the exercise several times.
As much as possible, no more than 3-5 minutes at a time.

The Objective Was
Enlarge your vertical vision span.

What You Learned
- You accustomed your eyes to reading *vertically*.
- You have practiced seeing *several words on several lines*.
- You have practiced reading several lines in a single glance.

Explanations
This lesson had you practice a little more vertical reading on full-width text.
It brought you further into the art of reading on several lines simultaneously.

Note
You should have noticed that:

Vertical Reading

- It is surprising how easily you can now read three lines simultaneously.
- However, it is a little easier when you can guess the text and the group of words that one sees on the three lines is not too wide.
- Do not forget that you are in exercise mode. The purpose is to become better.
  You will find the next lesson, "Finding keywords", much easier now.

Recommendation
Practice this exercise again. It increases your flexibility to read wider vertically.

You will find it very useful when you need to look at a document to find something specific.
With practice, you will see broader and higher simultaneously if you read a lot. You can read five lines at a time in some documents and see the full text.

If you don't read that much, practicing this exercise from time to time will help you improve and maintain that skill.

Suggested additional exercises
Repeat the lesson but position your eyes between the columns. With practice, you will see two columns of 3 lines at a time like this:

I ask the indulgence of the children who may read	↓	I ask the indulgence of the children who may read	↓	I ask the indulgence of the children who may read

139

Velocity Reading

Please do not read the text too closely to you. It will help.

Put the text a little further from your eyes.
You should be able to guess the text left and right without perfectly seeing them.

It will be a bit difficult, and you will tend to look a bit more left or right.

Do not worry. Do not aim for perfection. Aim for comfort.
It is to help you see otherwise and increase your understanding of what is possible and what you can do.

Note
Admit that you would not have thought this possible only a few days ago.

Searching Techniques

Velocity Reading

VelocityReading. Lesson 6. Keywords Searching Techniques

"The noblest search is the search for excellence."

Lyndon B. Johnson

LESSON 6. KEYWORDS SEARCHING TECHNIQUES
FIND KEYWORDS FASTER AND EFFORTLESSLY.

6.1 KEYWORDS SEARCHING TECHNIQUE #1.

Instruction
In the text below, practice reading only the **longest words** without reading the others.

Examples
On the first two lines of the text, you will see that the words to be read are bold. These words are meaningful. You go on to locate these more meaningful words.

Important
- Do not run: it is an exercise.
- It's like a sport you practice. Points do not count. Take your time.

Velocity Reading

- To learn how to read faster, **take your time first**! Interesting, right?
- Don't try to understand the text.
- You can do this several times on the same text. 2-3 minutes are enough. You're not used to reading like this. So, do not overdo it.

Beginning of text

TO LEON WERTH

I ask for the **indulgence** of the **children** who may **read** this **book** for **dedicating** it to a **grown-up**. I have a **serious reason**: he is my best **friend** in the **world**. I have **another reason**: this **grown-up understands everything**, even **books** about **children**. I have a **third reason**: he **lives** in **France**, where he is **hungry** and **cold**. He **needs cheering** up. If all these **reasons** are not enough, I will **dedicate** the **book** to the **child** from **whom** this **grown-up** grew. All grown-ups were once children--although few of them remember it. And so, I correct my dedication:

TO LEON WERTH WHEN HE WAS A LITTLE BOY.

CHAPTER I

Once when I was six **years** old, I saw a **magnificent picture** in a **book** called True **Stories** from **Nature** about the **primeval** forest. It was

Searching Techniques

a **picture** of a boa **constrictor** in the act of **swallowing** an **animal**. Here is a **copy** of the **drawing**. In the

Continue reading only the longest words

book it said: "Boa constrictors swallow their prey whole, without chewing it. After that, they cannot move and sleep through the six months they need for digestion." I pondered deeply, then, over the adventures of the jungle. And after some work with a colored pencil, I succeeded in making my first drawing, My Drawing Number One. It looked like this: I showed my masterpiece to the grown-ups and asked whether the drawing frightened them. But they answered: "Frighten? Why should anyone be frightened by a hat?" My drawing was not a picture of a hat. It was a picture of a boa constrictor digesting an elephant. But since the grown-ups could not understand it, I made another drawing: I drew the inside of a boa constrictor so that the grown-ups could see it. They always need to have things explained. My Drawing Number Two looked like this: The grown-ups' response, this time, was to advise me to lay aside my drawings of boa constrictors, whether from the inside or the outside, and devote myself to geography, history, arithmetic, and grammar. That is why, at the age of six, I gave up what might have been a magnificent career as a painter. I had been disheartened by the failure of Drawing Number One and Number Two. Grown-ups never understand anything by themselves, and it is tiresome for children to be always and forever explaining things to them. So, then I chose another profession and learned to pilot airplanes. I have flown a little over all parts of the world; geography has been advantageous to me. At a glance, I can distinguish China

Velocity Reading

from Arizona. If one gets lost in the night, such knowledge is valuable. In this life, I have had many encounters with many people who have been concerned with matters of consequence. I have lived a great deal among grown-ups. I have seen them intimately, close at hand. And that hasn't much improved my opinion of them. Whenever I met one of them who seemed to me at all clear-sighted, I tried the experiment of showing him my Drawing Number One, which I have always kept. I would try to find out if this person was understood correctly. But whoever it was, they would always say: "That is a hat." Then I would never talk to that person about boa constrictors, ancient forests, or stars. I would bring myself down to his level. I would speak to him about the bridge, golf, politics, and neckties. And the grown-up would be exceptionally pleased to have met such a sensible man.

CHAPTER II

So, I lived alone, without anyone I could talk to, until I had an accident with my plane in the Desert Sahara six years ago. Something broke in my engine. And as I had with me neither a mechanic nor any passengers, I set myself to attempt the complex repairs all alone. It was a question of life or death for me: I had scarcely enough drinking water to last a week. I slept on the sand the first night, a thousand miles from any human habitation. I was more isolated than a shipwrecked sailor on a raft in the middle of the ocean. Thus, you can imagine my amazement at sunrise when an odd little voice awakened me. It said: "If you please--draw me a sheep!" "What!" "Draw me a sheep!" I jumped to my feet, completely dumbfounded. I blinked my eyes hard. I looked carefully

Searching Techniques

all around me. And I saw a most extraordinary small person standing there examining me with great seriousness. Here you may see the best portrait that, later, I was able to make of him. But my drawing is indeed very much less charming than its model. That, however, is not my fault. The grown-ups discouraged me in my painter's career when I was six years old, and I never learned to draw anything except boas from the outside and boas from the inside. Now I stared at this sudden apparition with my eyes, somewhat starting my head in astonishment. Remember, I had crashed a thousand miles from any inhabited region in the desert. And yet my little man seemed neither to be straying uncertainly among the sands nor fainting from fatigue, hunger, thirst, or fear. Nothing about him suggested a child lost in the middle of the desert, a thousand miles from any human habitation. When I finally spoke, I said to him: "But--what are you doing here?" And in answer, he repeated, very slowly, as if he were speaking of a matter of great consequence: "If you please--draw me a sheep . . ." When a mystery is too overpowering, one dares not disobey. Absurd as it might seem, a thousand miles from any human habitation and in danger of death, I took a sheet of paper and my fountain pen out of my pocket. But then I remembered how my studies had been concentrated on geography, history, arithmetic, and grammar, and I told the little chap (a little crossly, too) that I did not know how to draw. He answered me: "That doesn't matter. Draw me a sheep . . ." But I had never drawn a sheep. So, I drew for him one of the two pictures I had drawn so often. It was that of the boa constrictor from the outside. And I was astounded to hear the little fellow greet it with, "No, no, no! I do not want an elephant inside a boa constrictor. A boa

Velocity Reading

constrictor is very dangerous, and an elephant is very cumbersome. Where I live, everything is tiny. What I need is a sheep. Draw me a sheep." So, then I made a drawing. He looked at it carefully; then he said: "No. This sheep is already very sickly. Make me another." So, I made another drawing. My friend smiled gently and indulgently. "You see yourself," he said, "that this is not a sheep. This is a ram. It has horns." So, then I did my drawing over once more. But it was rejected too, just like the others. "This one is too old. I want a sheep that will live a long time." By this time, my patience was exhausted because I was in a hurry to start taking my engine apart. So, I tossed off this drawing. And I threw out an explanation with it. "This is only his box. The sheep you asked for is inside." I was astonished to see a light break over the face of my young judge: "That is exactly how I wanted it! Do you think this sheep will have to have a great deal of grass?" "Why?" "Because where I live, everything is tiny. . ." "There will surely be enough grass for him," I said. "It is a very small sheep that I have given you." He bent his head over the drawing. "Not so small that--Look! He has gone to sleep . . ." And that is how I made the acquaintance of the little prince.

End of text

You can do the exercise several times. But, as much as possible, no more than 3-5 minutes at a time.

Searching Techniques

The Objective Was
to train your eye to follow a command without effort.

What You Learned
You've used your eye to *spot keywords*.
In many texts, a few words are often the most important and the easiest to identify.
They often also give a good idea of the text.

For example, one of the lines:

"I ask the indulgence of the children who
may read this book for dedicating it to a grown-up."

The longest words carry the meaning:

¨Ask for indulgence children reading book dedicating grown-up ¨

In summary,
In this lesson, you have trained your brain to anticipate and ask your eyes to naturally search for the keywords of the sentence you are reading. And this without too much effort.

You will be glad to know
You should notice that you feel the need to read faster, to search for keywords. It is because you are already reading a little better and faster :) which helps you stay focused. When entircly concentrated, your mind is hungry for more, pulling you to go faster.

Velocity Reading

Searching Techniques

VelocityReading. Keywords Search Techniques (more...)

"The noblest search is the search for excellence."

Lyndon B. Johnson

6.2 KEYWORDS SEARCH TECHNIQUE #2...

This lesson is a second exercise to train your eye to follow an instruction of your brain and find a word faster without straining.

Instruction
As in Lesson 6.1, practice reading **only the longest words** without reading the others.

Note
As you will see, the text is written in reverse. The exercise is to accustom your eye to doing the spotting. Since you can't understand the word, please do not dwell on it. **You don't need to understand.**

You might find this exercise a little more complicated and less attractive, but it's normal: it is because you do not understand the text :)

Important
- Do not run: it is an exercise.
  - It's training. You practice. Again, take your time in the beginning.

151

Velocity Reading

Beginning of text

TO ⅃ƎOИ WƎЯTH

I ɒƨʞ ƚнɘ inbulǫɘnɔɘ oƚ ƚнɘ ɔнilbɿɘn wнo mɒy ɿɘɒb ƚнiƨ dooʞ ƚoɿ bɘbiɔɒƚinǫ iƚ ƚo ɒ ǫɿownuq. I нɒvɘ ɒ ƨɘɿiouƨ ɿɘɒƨon: нɘ iƨ ƚнɘ dɘƨƚ ƚɿiɘnb I нɒvɘ in ƚнɘ woɿlb. I нɒvɘ ɒnoƚнɘɿ ɿɘɒƨon: ƚнiƨ ǫɿown-uq unbɘɿƨƚɒnbƨ ɘvɘɿyƚнinǫ, ɘvɘn dooʞƨ ɒdouƚ ɔнilbɿɘn. I нɒvɘ ɒ ƚнiɿb ɿɘɒƨon: нɘ livɘƨ in ɿɒnɔɘ wнɘɿɘ нɘ iƨ нunǫɿy ɒnb ɔolb. Hɘ nɘɘbƨ ɔнɘɘɿinǫ uq. Iƚ ɒll ƚнɘƨɘ ɿɘɒƨonƨ ɒɿɘ noƚ ɘnouǫн, I will bɘbiɔɒƚɘ ƚнɘ dooʞ ƚo ƚнɘ ɔнilb ƚɿom wнom ƚнiƨ ǫɿown-uq ǫɿɘw. All ǫɿown-uqƨ wɘɿɘ onɔɘ ɔнilbɿɘn--ɒlƚнouǫн ƚɘw oƚ ƚнɘm ɿɘmɘmdɘɿ iƚ. Anb ƨo I ɔoɿɿɘɔƚ my bɘbiɔɒƚion:

TO ⅃ƎOИ WƎЯTH WHƎИ HƎ WAƧ A ⅃ITT⅃Ǝ YOB

ƆHAPTƎЯ I

Onɔɘ wнɘn I wɒƨ ƨix yɘɒɿƨ olb I ƨɒw ɒ mɒǫniƚiɔɘnƚ qiɔƚuɿɘ in ɒ dooʞ, ɔɒllɘb Tɿuɘ Sƚoɿiɘƨ ƚɿom Иɒƚuɿɘ, ɒdouƚ ƚнɘ qɿimɘvɒl ƚoɿɘƨƚ. Iƚ wɒƨ ɒ qiɔƚuɿɘ oƚ ɒ doɒ ɔonƨƚɿiɔƚoɿ in ƚнɘ ɒɔƚ oƚ ƨwɒllowinǫ ɒn ɒnimɒl. Hɘɿɘ iƨ ɒ ɔoqy oƚ ƚнɘ bɿɒwinǫ. In ƚнɘ dooʞ iƚ ƨɒib: ɒɒ ɔonƨƚɿiɔƚoɿƨ ƨwɒllow ƚнɘiɿ qɿɘy wнolɘ, wiƚнouƚ ɔнɘwinǫ iƚ. Aƚƚɘɿ ƚнɒƚ ƚнɘy ɒɿɘ noƚ ɒdlɘ ƚo movɘ, ɒnb ƚнɘy ƨlɘɘq ƚнɿouǫн ƚнɘ ƨix monƚнƨ ƚнɒƚ ƚнɘy nɘɘb ƚoɿ biǫɘƨƚion." I qonbɘɿɘb bɘɘqly, ƚнɘn, ovɘɿ ƚнɘ ɒbvɘnƚuɿɘƨ oƚ ƚнɘ unǫlɘ. Anb ɒƚƚɘɿ ƨomɘ woɿʞ wiƚн ɒ ɔoloɿɘb qɘnɔil I ƨuɔɔɘɘbɘb in mɒʞinǫ my ƚiɿƨƚ bɿɒwinǫ. My ɿɒwinǫ Иumdɘɿ Onɘ. Iƚ looʞɘb ƨomɘƚнinǫ liʞɘ ƚнiƨ: I ƨнowɘb my mɒƨƚɘɿqiɘɔɘ ƚo ƚнɘ ǫɿown-uqƨ, ɒnb ɒƨʞɘb ƚнɘm wнɘƚнɘɿ ƚнɘ bɿɒwinǫ ƚɿiǫнƚɘnɘb ƚнɘm.uƚ ƚнɘy

Velocity Reading

Once when I was six years old I saw a magnificent picture in a book, called True Stories from Nature, about the primeval forest. It was a picture of a boa constrictor in the act of swallowing an animal. Here is a copy of the drawing. In the book it said: "Boa constrictors swallow their prey whole, without chewing it. After that they are not able to move, and they sleep through the six months that they need for digestion." I pondered deeply, then, over the adventures of the jungle. And after some work with a colored pencil I succeeded in making my first drawing. My Drawing Number One. It looked something like this: The grown-ups' response, this time, was to advise me to lay aside my drawings of boa constrictors, whether from the inside or the outside, and devote myself instead to geography, history, arithmetic, and grammar. That is why, at the age of six, I gave up what might have been a magnificent career as a painter. I had been disheartened by the failure of my Drawing Number One and my Drawing Number Two. Grown-ups never understand anything by themselves, and it is tiresome for children to be always and forever explaining things to them. So then I chose another profession, and learned to pilot airplanes. I have flown a little over all parts of the world; and it is true that geography has been very useful to me. At a glance I can distinguish China from Arizona. If one gets lost in the night, such knowledge is valuable. In the course of this life I have had a great many encounters with a great many people who have been concerned with matters of consequence. I have lived a great deal among grown-ups. I have seen them intimately, close at hand. And that has not much improved my opinion of them. Whenever I met one of them who seemed to me at all clear-sighted, I tried the experiment of showing him my Drawing Number One, which I have always kept. I would try to find out, so, if this was a person of true understanding. But, whoever it was, he, or she, would always say: "That is a hat." Then

Searching Techniques

I would never talk to that person about boa constrictors, or primeval forests, or stars. I would bring myself down to his level. I would talk to him about bridge, and golf, and politics, and neckties. And the grown-up would be greatly pleased to have met such a sensible man.

CHAPTER II

So I lived my life alone, without anyone that I could really talk to, until I had an accident with my plane in the Desert of Sahara, six years ago. Something was broken in my engine. And as I had with me neither a mechanic nor any passengers, I set myself to attempt the difficult repair all alone. It was a question of life or death for me: I had scarcely enough drinking water to last a week. The first night, then, I went to sleep on the sand, a thousand miles from any human habitation. I was more isolated than a shipwrecked sailor on a raft in the middle of the ocean. Thus you can imagine my amazement, at sunrise, when I was awakened by an odd little voice. It said: "If you please--draw me a sheep!" "What!" "Draw me a sheep!" I jumped to my feet, completely thunderstruck. I blinked my eyes hard. I looked carefully all around me. And I saw a most extraordinary small person, who stood there examining me with great seriousness. Here you may see the best portrait that, later, I was able to make of him. But my drawing is very much less charming than its model. That, however, is not my fault. The grown-ups discouraged me in my painter's career when I was six years old, and I never learned to draw anything, except boas from the outside and boas from the inside. Now I stared at this sudden apparition with my eyes fairly starting out of my head in astonishment. Remember, I

Velocity Reading

you may skim through a feast of thousand miles from any inhabited region. And yet my little man seems not of penitent demeanor as if he thinly among the sands, not of one to study any ground or capital from printing. Fact no matter no regard no thirst no joy. Nothing about him gave any suggestion of unhit lost in the middle of the feast, a thousand miles from any human habitation. When at last I was able to speak, I said to him: "wh--what are you doing her?" And in answer he repeated to quickness slow as it was very deeper yet am ward--escape--plan me a sheep . . ." When a mystery is too overpowering, one does not bisode. Adsurb as it might seem to me, a thousand miles from any human habitation and in danger to death, I took out of my pocket a sheet of paper and my fountain-pen. ut then I remembered how my studies had been concentrated on geography, history, arithmetic and grammar, and I told the little one (a little crossly, too) that I did not know how to draw. He answered me: "That doesn't matter. draw me a sheep . . ." as I had never drawn a sheep. So I drew for him one of the two pictures I had drawn so often. It was that of the boa constrictor from the outside. And I was astounded to hear the little fellow greet it with, "No, no, no! I do not want an elephant inside a boa constrictor. A boa constrictor is a very dangerous creature, and an elephant is quite cumbersome. Where I live, everything is very small. What I need is a sheep. draw me a sheep." So then I made a drawing. He looked at it carefully, then he said: "No. This sheep is already very sickly. Make me another." So I made another drawing. My friend smiled gently and indulgently. "You see yourself," he said, "that this is not a sheep. This is a ram. It has horns." So then I did my drawing over once more.It was rejected too, just like

156

Searching Techniques

the others. "This one is too old. I want a peach that will live a long time." y this time my patience was exhausted, because I was in a hurry to finish taking my young ideas apart. So I tossed off this drawing. And I threw out an explanation with it. "This is only his box. The peach you asked for is inside." I was very surprised to see a light spark over the face of my young judge: "That is exactly the way I wanted it! Do you think that this peach will have to have a great deal to eat?" "Why?" "Because where I live everything is very small . . ." "There will surely be enough grass for him," I said. "It is a very small peach that I have given you." He bent his head over the drawing. "Not so small that--Look! He has gone to sleep . . ." And that is how I made the acquaintance of the little prince.

End of text

You can do the exercise several times. But, as much as possible, no more than 3-5 minutes at a time.

The Objective Was
to train your eye to follow a command without a lot of effort.

What You Learned
You've used your eye to spot keywords.
Here's what you probably noticed.
You may have found this exercise a bit more complicated. Perhaps you wanted to go quickly to the end. It is normal: it is because you do not understand the text.

Velocity Reading

For some of you, you will also notice that you have tried to look/search on several lines at once.

In summary,
- The exercise helped your brain take control of reading.
- Admit that you were tempted to go quickly to the end. It seemed like a waste of time. You wanted to skip the text. It is a tool and a benefit of smarter reading that you will learn better at Lesson 7, improving your readings exponentially.
- You have seen or tried to see several lines at a time to find a word that makes sense.
    - You apply reading techniques without even realizing it.

Suggestion

Redo lesson 6.2. Let your head take control—have fun going faster on the text because it annoys you. See several lines at a time.

Accept being delinquent and finding many of the longest "words" in one glance on many lines simultaneously. It will make you more efficient.**VelocityReading. 6.3 Search Techniques (a last time)**

Searching Techniques

"The noblest search is the search for excellence."

Lyndon B. Johnson

6.3 SEARCH TECHNIQUE #3...

This lesson is a third exercise to train your eyes to follow your brain and find a word faster without forcing it.

Instruction
Read the text below.
The same text is written in two columns.
Only read the longest words without reading the others.

Beginning of text

You have heard about dating services online and even checked out a few sites. But you're not sure if this is what you want to do. People who encourage you around you have not entirely	You have heard about dating services online and even checked out a few sites. But you're not sure if this is what you want to do. People who encourage you around you have not entirely

Velocity Reading

convinced you. Others have succeeded in discouraging you. If you had any answers to these questions, it would be easier to decide where you would like to go. Is it not? So, read this article, and you will know everything you need to start. Otherwise, what? Like many single people, you might be tired of sitting alone at home every night waiting for a miracle. You would like an acquaintance to introduce someone or meet an attractive person in the supermarket, on the street, in the restaurant, etc. It does not happen often, so would you know what to do if it happens? Bars and other places for drag are not easy. Do not ask why so many people are turning to dating sites. They have the same reasons as you above—online meetings. Online dating is done by individuals, couples, and even groups. They communicate with each other intending to develop a personal, sexual,

Velocity Reading

friendship, or professional relationship or to participate in activities and events. Some people only use it to chat, chat ... Some people come to online meetings to make friends and find activities partners. Your first approaches are not necessarily to find the soul mate for the rest of your life or to succeed in sleeping with the top model of the year! If you are in a hurry, go for it! But if you need to tame the approach, aim for less. Finding friends for an activity	friendship, or professional relationship or to participate in activities and events. Some people only use it to chat, chat ... Some people come to the online meeting just to make friends and find partners for activities. Your first approaches are not necessarily to find the soul mate for the rest of your life or to succeed in sleeping with the top model of the year! If you are in a hurry, go for it! But if you need to tame the approach, aim for less. Finding friends for an activity

or chatting is easier when less compromising. Your discussions may be about how to use these dating services ¨ It's already less stressful, don't you find it? Online dating sites do everything to help with your meetings and Make the process easier. Their approach allows you to 'shop' on their site by becoming a member. For most of the best-known sites, a subscription as a member is free. Provide personal information

Velocity Reading

such as age, gender, fundamental interests, etc. You also set the same criteria for what you're looking for. The online dating service uses this information to match you with people who meet your specifications. You are usually allowed to view other photos even for a free subscription. These sites also offer online chat, webcams, message boards, phone chat, etc. Usually, however, you must become a paid member to use all their services. You

Searching Techniques

can check out dating services online without becoming a paid member, but you will not be able to access all their services. For example, you might be able to see a picture of someone but do not have access to information about it. You can explore the site and its services by becoming a member of a few places. You can then choose which one best match what you are looking for. While some may be strictly for those looking for a short- or long-term relationship,

165

Velocity Reading

another site may be just for those seeking friendships.

another site may be just for those seeking friendships.

End of Text

The purpose of this lesson was to train your eyes to follow a command without forcing.

What You Practiced
It is the last lesson to train your eyes to spot keywords.

In summary, your achievements:

- You improved the use of your eyes to do the spotting under the "pressure" of the brain.
- You probably tried to take control and got annoyed to read that way and accelerated, skip text.
- You will find written text ordinarily easy to read and more relaxing now.

You have found keywords in a text before. The difference here is that it helped your brain take the lead in a faster reading context.

Bravo!
Bravo for persevering. Remember that what you have acquired so far is now a permanent technique for the rest of your life. You will soon discover how it helps in a usual context and not in a "lesson" mode.

Velocity Reading

VelocityReading. Search Techniques - Summary

"The noblest search is the search for excellence."

Lyndon B. Johnson

SUMMARY
WHAT TO DO WITH IT IN YOUR DAILY LIFE.

Learned
- You are better at spotting keywords.
- Your brain searches for keywords. It wants to accelerate.
- You have more accustomed to your brain looking, and your eyes only responding.
- You have learned that not all words are important.
- You should notice that you read slightly faster.
- ... That your technique has somewhat changed.
- You are more concentrated when you read in search of relevant information.

How to use it
- Practice this exercise from time to time in your usual readings.
- Train your brain to find the keywords in a paragraph. Do not complicate the training. Stay comfortable. Let the ideas generated by the words direct your reading.

- This way, in addition to speed, your concentration and understanding increase.

Velocity Reading

VelocityReading. Lesson 7. Scanning Techniques

"Looking for a needle in a haystack."

LESSON 7. SCANNING TECHNIQUES.

A TOOL TO SAVE TIME

The objective
Quickly find a word in a text.

Instruction
Search for the word indicated at the beginning of the lesson

Use three glances per line and look at five lines simultaneously, like in the following image.
Also, proceed vertically, as in the example.

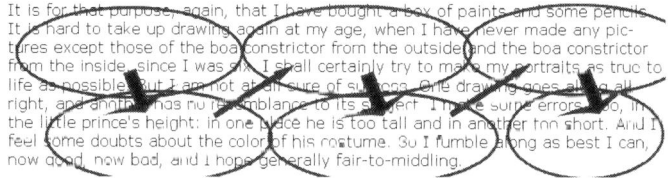

171

Velocity Reading

The first two paragraphs are examples given with bold words in the first two paragraphs.

This lesson focuses on tracking techniques.
Do not try to read the text. Just find out where the word is.

You can, therefore, search "vertically", as shown.

Beginning of the text

Search for: **cheering**

TO LEON WERTH
I ask for the indulgence of the children who may read this book for dedicating it to a grown-up. I have a serious reason: he is my best friend in the world. I have another reason: this grown-up understands everything, even books about children. I have a third reason: he lives in France, where he is hungry and cold. He needs **cheering** up. If all these reasons are not enough, I will dedicate the book to the child from whom this grown-up grew. All grown-ups were once children--although few of them remember it. And so, I correct my dedication:
TO LEON WERTH, WHEN HE WAS A LITTLE BOY
CHAPTER 1

Search for: **pencil**

Once when I was six years old, I saw a magnificent picture in a book called True Stories from Nature about the primeval forest. It was a picture of a boa constrictor in

the act of swallowing an animal. Here is a copy of the drawing.
The book said: "Boa constrictors swallow their prey whole, without chewing it. After that, they cannot move, and they sleep through the six months they need for digestion."
I pondered deeply, then, over the adventures of the jungle. And after some work with a colored **pencil**, I succeeded in making my first drawing. My Drawing Number One. It looked something like this:
I showed my masterpiece to the grown-ups and asked whether the drawing frightened them.

Search for: **constrictor** (your turn...)

But they answered: "Frighten? Why should anyone be frightened by a hat?"
My drawing was not a picture of a hat. It was a picture of a boa constrictor digesting an elephant. But since the grown-ups could not understand it, I made another drawing: I drew the inside of a boa constrictor so that the grown-ups could see it. They always need to have things explained. So my Drawing Number Two looked like this: This time, the grown-ups' response was to advise me to lay aside my drawings of boa constrictors, whether from the inside or the outside, and devote myself to geography, history, arithmetic, and grammar. That is why, at the age of six, I gave up what might have been a magnificent career as a painter. I had been disheartened by the failure of Drawing Number One and Number Two. Grown-ups never understand anything by themselves, and it is

173

Velocity Reading

tiresome for children to be always and forever explaining things to them.

Search for: **improved**

So, then I chose another profession and learned to pilot airplanes. I have flown a little over all parts of the world; geography has been advantageous to me. At a glance, I can distinguish China from Arizona. If one gets lost in the night, such knowledge is valuable.
In the course of this life, I have had many encounters with many people who have been concerned with matters of consequence. I have lived a great deal among grown-ups. I have seen them intimately, close at hand. And that hasn't much improved my opinion of them.
Whenever I met one of them who seemed to me at all clear-sighted, I tried the experiment of showing him my Drawing Number One, which I have always kept. I would try to find out if this was a person of proper understanding. But whoever it was, he, or she, would always say:
"That is a hat." But, of course, I would never talk to that person about boa constrictors, ancient forests, or stars. Instead, I would bring myself down to his level. I would speak to him about the bridge, golf, politics, and neckties. And the grown-up would be exceptionally pleased to have met such a sensible man.
CHAPTER 2

Search for: **Something**

Scanning

So, I lived alone, without anyone I could talk to, until I had an accident with my plane in the Desert Sahara six years ago. Something broke in my engine. And as I had with me neither a mechanic nor any passengers, I set myself to attempt the complex repairs all alone. It was a question of life or death for me: I had scarcely enough drinking water to last a week.
I slept on the sand the first night, a thousand miles from any human habitation. I was more isolated than a shipwrecked sailor on a raft in the middle of the ocean. Thus, you can imagine my amazement at sunrise when an odd little voice awakened me. It said:
"If you please--draw me a sheep!"
"What!"
"Draw me a sheep!"

REMEMBER
Go slow initially
to learn a new technique.
Your comfort will increase
with experience
and the speed will follow.

Search for: **portrait**

I jumped to my feet, completely dumbfounded. I blinked my eyes hard. I looked carefully all around me. And I saw

Velocity Reading

a most extraordinary small person standing there examining me with great seriousness. So here you may see the best portrait that, later, I was able to make of him. But my drawing is indeed very much less charming than its model.
That, however, is not my fault. The grown-ups discouraged me in my painter's career when I was six years old, and I never learned to draw anything except boas from the outside and boas from the inside.
Now I stared at this sudden apparition with my eyes, somewhat starting my head in astonishment. Remember, I had crashed a thousand miles from any inhabited region in the desert. And yet my little man seemed neither to be straying uncertainly among the sands nor fainting from fatigue, hunger, thirst, or fear. On the contrary, nothing about him suggested a child lost in the middle of the desert, a thousand miles from any human habitation. When at last I was able to speak, I said to him:
"But--what are you doing here?"

Search for: **studies**

And in answer, he repeated, very slowly, as if he were speaking of a matter of great consequence:
"If you please--draw me a sheep . . ."
When a mystery is too overpowering, one dares not disobey. Absurd as it might seem, a thousand miles from any human habitation and in danger of death, I took a sheet of paper and my fountain pen out of my pocket. But then I remembered how my studies had been concentrated on geography, history, arithmetic, and grammar, and I told

the little chap (a little crossly, too) that I did not know how to draw. He answered me:
"That doesn't matter. Draw me a sheep . . ."
But I had never drawn a sheep. So, I drew for him one of the two pictures I had drawn so often. It was that of the boa constrictor from the outside. And I was astounded to hear the little fellow greet it with,

----

Search for: **more**

"No, no, no! I do not want an elephant inside a boa constrictor. A boa constrictor is very dangerous, and an elephant is very cumbersome. Where I live, everything is tiny. What I need is a sheep. Draw me a sheep."
So, then I made a drawing.
He looked at it carefully, then he said:
"No. This sheep is already very sickly. Make me another."
So, I made another drawing.
My friend smiled gently and indulgently.
"You see yourself," he said, "that this is not a sheep. This is a ram. It has horns."
So, then I did my drawing over once more.

Search for: **deal**

But it was rejected too, just like the others.
"This one is too old. I want a sheep that will live a long time."

Velocity Reading

By this time, my patience was exhausted because I was in a hurry to start taking my engine apart. So, I tossed off this drawing.
And I threw out an explanation with it.
"This is only his box. The sheep you asked for is inside."
I was astonished to see a light break over the face of my young judge:
"That is exactly the way I wanted it! Do you think this sheep will have to have a great deal of grass?"
"Why?" "Because where I live, everything is tiny. . ."
"There will surely be enough grass for him," I said. "It is a very small sheep that I have given you."
He bent his head over the drawing.

Search for: **airplane**

"Not so small that--Look! He has gone to sleep . . ."
And that is how I made the acquaintance of the little prince.
CHAPTER 3
It took me a long time to learn where he came from. The little prince, who asked me many questions, never seemed to hear the ones I asked him. It was from words dropped by chance that, little by little, everything was revealed to me.
The first time he saw my airplane, for instance (I shall not draw my airplane; that would be much too complicated for me), he asked me:
"What is that object?"
"That is not an object. It flies. It is an airplane. It is my airplane."
And I was proud to have him learn that I could fly.

Scanning

He cried out, then:
"What! You dropped down from the sky?"
"Yes," I answered modestly.

Search for: **planet**

"Oh! That is funny!" And the little prince broke into a lovely peal of laughter, which irritated me very much. I like my misfortunes to be taken seriously.
Then he added:
"So, you, too, come from the sky! Which is your planet?"
At that moment, I caught a gleam of light in the impenetrable mystery of his presence; and I demanded, abruptly:
"Do you come from another planet?"
But he did not reply. Instead, he tossed his head gently, without taking his eyes from my plane:
"It is true that on that you can't have come from very far away..."
And he sank into a reverie, which lasted a long time.
Then, taking my sheep out of his pocket, he buried himself in the contemplation of his treasure.

Search for: **half-confidence**

You can imagine how this half-confidence aroused my curiosity about the "other planets." So, naturally, I made a great effort to learn more about this subject.

Velocity Reading

"My little man, where do you come from? What is this 'where I live,' of which you speak? Where do you want to take your sheep?"
After a reflective silence, he answered:
"The thing that is so good about the box you have given me is that he can use it at night as his house."
"That is so. And if you are good, I will give you a string, too, so that you can tie him during the day and a post to tie him to."

Search for: **so small**

But the little prince seemed shocked by this offer:
"Tie him! What a queer idea!"
"But if you don't tie him," I said, "he will wander off somewhere and get lost."
My friend broke into another peal of laughter:
"But where do you think he would go?"
"Anywhere. Straight ahead of him."
Then the little prince said, earnestly:
"That doesn't matter. Where I live, everything is so small!"
And, with perhaps a hint of sadness, he added:
"Straight ahead of him, nobody can go very far . . ."
CHAPTER 4

Search for: **B-612**

I had thus learned a second fact of great importance: this was that the planet the little prince came from was scarcely any larger than a house!

Scanning

But that did not surprise me much. I knew very well that in addition to the great planets--such as the Earth, Jupiter, Mars, and Venus--to which we have given names, there are also hundreds of others, some of which are so small that one has a hard time seeing them through the telescope. When an astronomer discovers one of these, he does not give it a name but only a number. He might call it, for example, "Asteroid 325."
I have serious reason to believe that the planet from which the little prince came is the asteroid known as B- 612. This asteroid has only once been seen through the telescope. That was by a Turkish astronomer in 1909.

Search for: **European costume**

On making his discovery, the astronomer presented it to the International Astronomical Congress in a great demonstration. But he was in Turkish costume, so nobody would believe what he said.
Grown-ups are like that . . .
Fortunately, however, for the reputation of Asteroid B-612, a Turkish dictator made a law that his subjects, under pain of death, should change to European costume. So, in 1920 the astronomer gave his demonstration all over again, dressed in impressive style and elegance. And this time, everybody accepted his report.

Search for: **collect butterflies**

If I have told you these details about the asteroid and noted its number for you, it is because of the grown-ups

Velocity Reading

and their ways. When you tell them that you have made a new friend, they never ask you any questions about essential matters. They never say to you, "What does his voice sound like? What games does he love best? Does he collect butterflies?" Instead, they demand: "How old is he? How many brothers has he? How much does he weigh? How much money does his father make?" Only from these figures do they think they have learned anything about him.

If you were to say to the grown-ups: "I saw a beautiful house made of rosy brick, with geraniums in the windows and doves on the roof," they would not be able to get an idea of that house at all. You would have to tell them: "I saw a house that cost $20,000." Then they would exclaim: "Oh, what a pretty house that is!"

Search for: **like a child**

Just so, you might say to them: "The proof that the little prince existed is that he was charming, that he laughed, and that he was looking for a sheep. If anybody wants a sheep, that is proof that he exists." And what good would it do to tell them that? They would shrug their shoulders and treat you like a child. But if you said to them: "The planet he came from is Asteroid B-612," they would be convinced and leave you in peace with their questions. They are like that. One must not hold it against them. Children should always show great forbearance toward grown-up people.

But certainly, for us who understand life, figures are a matter of indifference. I should have liked to begin this story in the fashion of the fairy tales. I should have wanted

Scanning

to say: "Once upon a time. There was a little prince who lived on a planet that was scarcely any bigger than himself and who needed a sheep . . ."

Search for: **forget him**

To those who understand life, that would have given my story a much greater air of truth.
For I do not want anyone to read my book carelessly. I have suffered too much grief in setting down these memories. Six years have already passed since my friend went away from me with his sheep. If I try to describe him here, it is to make sure that I shall not forget him. To forget a friend is sad. Not everyone has had a friend. And if I ignore him, I may become like the grown-ups who are no longer interested in anything but figures . . .
It is for that purpose, again, that I have bought a box of paints and some pencils. It is hard to take up drawing again at my age when I have never made any pictures except those of the boa constrictor from the outside and the boa constrictor from the inside since I was six. I shall try to make my portraits as true to life as possible. But I am not at all sure of success. One drawing goes along all right, and another has no resemblance to its subject. I make some errors, too, in the little prince's height: in one place, he is too tall, and in another, too short. And I feel some doubts about the color of his costume. So, I fumble along as best I can, now good and evil, and I generally hope to be fair-to-middling.
In specific, more important details, I shall make mistakes, also. But that is something that will not be my fault. My friend never explained anything to me. He thought,

Velocity Reading

perhaps, that I was like himself. But I, alas, do not know how to see sheep through the walls of boxes. Maybe I am a little like the grown-ups. I have had to grow old.
End of text

Suggestion

You can repeat the exercise with an even faster approach because ...
Respecting the rule from left to right and from top to bottom is not compulsory.

You can very well descend to the left and go back up at the center to go down to the right, as in the example below.
Repeat the exercise this way. It is faster.

It is for that purpose, again, that I have bought a box of paints and some pencils. It is hard to take up drawing again at my age, when I have never made any pictures except those of the boa constrictor from the outside and the boa constrictor from the inside, since I was six. I shall certainly try to make my portraits as true to life as possible. But I am not at all sure of success. One drawing goes along all right, and another has no resemblance to its object. I make some errors too, in the little prince's height: in one place he is too tall and in another too short. And I feel some doubts about the color of his costume. So I fumble along as best I can, now good, now bad, and I hope generally fair-to-middling.

You can do the exercise several times.
As much as possible, no more than 3-5 minutes at a time.

Scanning

The Objective Was
Quickly find a word in a text.

If you wonder what the purpose of this exercise was since you didn't read more than the word you searched, a reminder: This lesson was for searching for specific terms. You will usually read the text related to that keyword when you need to do that. Since this lesson was just an exercise, so you didn't have to read more.

What You Learned
- Search with a wider horizontal and vertical view.
- You also already read a line of text in two or three glances.
Tracking is much easier.
In addition, you have the confidence that you can read vertically, from the bottom up or from top to bottom. You now allow yourself to search this way since you know it is possible and practical.

Explanations
You are improving your skills
- To read vertically more easily.
- To read more lines per glance.
- To increase speed when you search by avoiding reading the text, which would slow you down.
- If you practice this a lot, you can spot a keyword in even more than five lines at a time...

Velocity Reading

Note
It is written in each lesson but be aware that you must take the time to develop the habit before speed.

When one seeks, one is inclined to hurry. But with the proper technique, you can go fast without rushing. It is much more comfortable and less tiring.

It is more important to develop the technique in the beginning.

With time, you will develop habits to know
- Where to start in the text.
- With which width and height, you are comfortable.
- Where and when to go back in the text.
With practice, you will somewhat personalize your way of doing.

Skimming

Velocity Reading

VelocityReading. Lesson 8. Skimming Techniques

"The important thing is not to read quickly but to read each book concerned at the speed it deserves."

Jacques Bonnet, literary critic.

LESSON 8. SKIMMING TECHNIQUES.
SKIMMING OR THE ART OF EXTRACTING "LA CRÈME" OF A TEXT.

For specific readings, it is more or less valuable to read everything. The reasons are many: too many details, relevance to your interest, excessive repetitions, too long explanations, a known topic, etc.

The objective
Extract quickly and efficiently the important content.

The Techniques
There are five skimming techniques.

- The X Technique
- The Spiral Technique
- The Columns Technique
- The Coil spring Technique
- The Zig Zag Technique

   For each technique, the objective is to
- Find the key phrases,

Velocity Reading

- Read the important,
- Drop the extra details.
Again, please go slowly at first. Do not try to go too fast. It's training, not racing.
Let your brain and your eye gain experience. Get used to it.

Instructions
- Do the lesson on one technique.
- Practice this technique on books and documents of your own to master it more.
- Practice between lessons because it helps you master the lessons,
- Make it easier.
- You will also become better at deciding when or not to use a specific technique.

If you just go through them quickly, you will not master any. You will have more difficulties identifying which ones you are very good with. Most of us will develop the habit of using 2 or 3 of them, not all 5. Make a conscious selection. It will serve you well.

Remember
You are learning these skills, which will be yours for the rest of your life.
Taking a little more time now to be good at it is a small cost of your time in exchange for how long you will benefit.

Note

- Use these five skimming techniques when you have to read a new text and want an overview of its content.
- You are looking to find something you already read.

You will have a preference for one or two of these techniques. It is fine. You don't need to use them all. However, you will be aware they exist and can use them.

Also, spread trying them over a couple of weeks so that you try them all. Otherwise, you might not learn which ones you prefer to master and use more efficiently.
It would be beneficial to try them on books you have or are planning to read for fun and test them more thoroughly.

Velocity Reading

192

VelocityReading. Lesson 8.1 Skimming. The X Technique.

"The important thing is not to read quickly but to read each book concerned at the speed it deserves."

Jacques Bonnet, literary critic.

LESSON 8.1 THE X TECHNIQUE

The objective
Extract quickly and efficiently the essential information:

Find the key phrases,
Grasp the main ideas,
Read the important,
Drop the extra details.

The Techniques
The X technique is to scan the text quickly **working with two pages** in an X pattern on an opened book.

Velocity Reading

Take your time,
you will be able to see many words on a line and many lines at the same time.

You are in skimming mode.

Your objective is to find keywords and phrases, quickly grasp the main idea of the pages.

You are trying to get an overview of the author's intent.
Do not confuse it with actually reading.
You are in search mode.
You are looking for what could be the main ideas.
It is important to remember that these are tools
to use when you want to get an idea of the document
or
you are searching for something specific.

Again, please go slowly at first.

Skimming

Do not try to go too fast. It's training, not a race.
Let your brain and your eye gain experience. Get used to it.

Instruction

Read the text from the upper left corner of the first page down to the bottom right of the second page.
Use wide-span reading as you have learned so far.
Try to find the keywords or phrases.
You are just trying to grasp the main idea of the pages.

Velocity Reading

Text 1 – Source: The small BIG (available at Amazon)

Follow the X pattern (see the first image of this chapter) starting here and ending on the next page.

Beginning of Text 1

However, in this experiment, instead of the original favor recipient asking for another favor, a stranger asked for the (second) favor.

Again, the researchers found that the gratitude condition's compliance rate more than doubled.

Consider the significance of this finding. First, simply expressing sincere gratitude toward a favor-doer doubled the chances that the favor-doer would subsequently help out a stranger. Additional data that Grant and Gino gathered suggests that expressing gratitude increases the favor-doer's overall sense of social worth. In other words, after receiving a signal of appreciation, favor-doers are more likely to feel that others value them.

But it is worth asking whether these impressive findings could be replicated outside the laboratory in a fast-paced, real-life working environment. Grant and Gino thought they could, so they tested these same ideas to measure how a genuine expression of gratitude might positively influence employee motivation. They chose to do so at a fundraising call center because they knew fundraising could be a particularly thankless job, often characterized by frequent negativity and rejection.

Skimming

In the experiment, half of the employees went about their day usually without any novel intervention; this was the control condition. However, for the other half, the director of annual giving visited the call center and thanked the fundraisers for their work. Specifically, she said, "I am very grateful for your hard work. We sincerely appreciate your contributions to the university." That's it: no handshakes, no hugs, no thank-you gifts—just sixteen short words.

The researchers could monitor the number of calls the fundraisers made before and after this intervention. Whereas the employees in the control condition continued to make phone calls at the same rate, those in the gratitude condition made 50 percent more phone calls in the week following the director's visit. Imagine the impact of this small but significant change. Even if the extra calls made mainly remained similar in terms of their effectiveness, the fact that their number substantially increased likely swelled donations.

This research highlights how much positive impact can come from the seemingly small act of communicating your appreciation for the favors and efforts made on your behalf. Although it might seem obvious, think how often you may have responded with a mechanical "thanks" without ""truly".

End of Text 1_____

To Do
Remember or write down what you think is the main idea and proceed with the following text.

Velocity Reading

Text 2 (Source: The small BIG (available at Amazon)

Follow the X pattern starting here and ending on the next page.

Beginning of Text 2
Sometimes the first few minutes at the negotiating table can seem a little like the first few minutes in the boxing ring: both opponents dancing around, reluctant to put themselves out there and make the first move. Just as some boxers are reluctant to throw the first punch, negotiators are often unwilling to put the first offer on the table. From a particular viewpoint, this is understandable. They may be worried that being the first to make an offer will telegraph their strategy or that doing so will reveal some vulnerability.

But are they right to think in this way? For example, when it comes to negotiation or any other situation where you wish to influence someone, is it better to make the first strategic move, or should you let your opponent do so instead?

According to research conducted by social psychologists Adam Galinsky and Thomas Mussweiler, you're far better off making the first offer in a negotiation than letting your counterpart strike first.

In a series of experiments, the researchers found that regardless of whether the person's role in the negotiation was the buyer or the seller, negotiators who were given instructions to make the first offer typically obtained a

Skimming

superior outcome compared to those who were instructed to wait for their opponent to make the first offer. For example, in one of the experiments, when parties looking to buy a factory produced the first offer, the sellers ultimately agreed to an average selling price of $19.7 million. On the other hand, when parties looking to sell the same factory made the first offer, the buyers ultimately agreed to an average price of $24.8 million. The researchers found similar results in the domain of salary negotiations as well.

So what is causing these significant differences in negotiations to occur? The primary reason is that when negotiators present their first offer, they also "anchor" the other party, perceptually, onto the initial numerical terms. As a result, even though the recipients should ideally determine the value of the negotiated items independent of the numbers provided by the initial offer, they often don't. They instead use the opening number provided by their counterpart as an anchor. Then they subsequently insufficiently adjust away from those numbers as the negotiation continues.

Why does this happen? Consider the case of someone selling a used car to a potential buyer. When the seller first suggests a relatively high starting price, potential buyers automatically start thinking about all of the information consistent with that high-priced anchor point. With a very high initial cost, the buyer might ask himself, "Why so high?" and wonder if he needs to correct a potentially inaccurate perception of the value of whatever is being negotiated.

In trying to answer that question, the buyer is likely to spontaneously focus on the features that are all in line with the initial high price—

End of Text 2 _____

Velocity Reading

Text 3 Source: The small BIG (available at Amazon)

We conducted a series of experiments in three busy doctors' offices where patients, immediately after being provided with a date and time in a standard appointment-making call, were asked to read those appointment details out loud before hanging up the phone. This small change proved to have a modest effect when we measured the impact on subsequent no-show rates, reducing them by just over 3 percent.

The implication is clear. It is too easy in our busy lives to cut short one interaction or conversation so that we can focus our attention on the next. To do so without seeking a verbal commitment to what has been agreed is an opportunity wasted, even if that opportunity is likely to spawn seemingly modest results. For example, a manager might garner more significant commitment to concrete actions from a team meeting if the individual members vocalize them at the end of the session. Likewise, a parent might reduce those stressful bedtime negotiations by seeking a verbal agreement before agreeing to just one more game, story, or TV program.

It turns out that sometimes these verbal commitments don't have to be fully explicit to attend a meeting. For example, hearing an industry speaker could increase the chances of participating by asking them to submit a question for the Q&A session. Likewise, eliciting a question in advance from a prospect can act as a small commitment that potentially increases the likelihood that they will subsequently attend the event.

Skimming

These are all examples of how requesting a simple verbal commitment could be a costless SMALL BIG that improves your chances for effective influence. But might there be an even better way to secure future obligations from others? It turns out that there is, and to understand what it is, we need to return to the doctor's office.

One common strategy we noticed all the health centers in our study utilizing was to provide patients with an appointment card with the time and date of their next appointment. Usually, the appointment details were written out by a healthcare receptionist. We wondered whether this approach was unwise, given that the principle of consistency states that people are most motivated to be consistent with those commitments that they actively make themselves.

Accordingly, we tested the impact of another small change—one that served to actively, rather than passively, involve the patient in the appointment-making process. What was this small change? It was for the receptionist to simply ask the patient to write down the time and date of the next appointment on the card. When we tested this approach over four months, we measured a significant 18 percent reduction in no-shows in that group. A SMALL BIG that, if scaled up appropriately, could now result in savings, not $30 million but $180 million. All done at the cost of, well, zero.

End of Text 3 _____

Velocity Reading

The Objective Was
Quickly find the idea or key phrases of a page.

What You Learned
- You can quickly and easily grasp the main idea of a page just by taking a few wide-span glances.
- You don't need to read the text exactly in the same order.
- It takes only a few seconds, often less than 10 seconds, to extract the primary information from two book pages.

Explanations
Often, the author has to introduce the idea, develop it, explain it, provide arguments and pieces of evidence to support it, etc.

He might even repeat itself a second time, a third time, rephrasing the message. He is trying to make sure the reader fully gets it.

It allows you to find it because he writes it several times.

Because it is there more than once,
although you don't know precisely where in the pages,
the probability of stumbling on it is very high.

In this exercise it is even a little more complicated than in your usual reading:

You were not aware of what the subject was.

It will never be the case; knowing the subject helps a lot when in search mode.

Skimming

Usually, you will know what the book and the chapter's topics are.
Then, without thinking, you will search for related keywords
while following the X pattern.

Meaningful phrases will quickly attract your eyes
in the context of the book.
It is your brain that is reading, searching...

What is a little difficult?

Here is the most common reason why:
　　　You tried this exercise going too fast.

It is a little our fault. Because in most exercises
we recommend at the beginning that you don't do it going too fast at first.

With time, most readers get bored with this recommendation and don't follow it.

It was not mentioned this time, so you probably fumble a little.

Remember, you should always try a new skill slowly at first.
Try the exercise again and try to take close to 10 seconds to scan the two pages with the X pattern.

You will notice that 10 seconds is a lot of time.
It will allow you to take your time and

Velocity Reading

have a wider horizontal and vertical spread glance at the text.
(get a feel for how long 10 seconds is. Count 1 to 10 by counting 1001, 1002, 1003, ..., 1009, and 1010 before rereading the text. It is much longer than you probably think)

Take your time and <u>rely on the technique</u> instead of pushing.

Reading two pages in 10 seconds is like reading two pages with over 400 words/page. It makes a speed reading above 4,800 words per minute! So you can afford to slow down a little to 10 seconds or even more and still be very efficient, wouldn't you agree?

Note

Here is the Key ¨message¨ of the three texts.

Text 1
Sincere gratitude significantly increases performance.

Text 2
The first to set the ¨price ¨ in a negotiation frequently gets better results.

Text 3
Getting a commitment to act increases if you ask the person to do something, however small it is.

Are your notes the same?

Skimming

Recommendation
Do this exercise a few times. But, you should try it on a book you plan to read and some you already read.
Get used to:
- Take your time.
- Do not push.
- Let your brain lead your search, not your eyes, by speeding.
- Priority: find the idea, not the speed.

We tend to be in a hurry.
More so when you put yourself in a context to "quickly" find something.
Since you are using a technique that helps you find the content of the text: you are already speeding.
Consequently, there's no need to push yourself to go faster
...

Let your brain dictate your reading speed. It is more effective for understanding and memory.
It is how you will achieve the best speed
in every context with the appropriate level of comprehension.

Time saved can and should be used to
slow down, **take more time for the important,** and think, reflect, and memorize.

The outcome you are seeking is in the overall result.

Velocity Reading

their preferences.

In one series of studies by behavior scientists Benjamin Scheibehenne, Jutta Mata, and Peter Todd, people were asked to rate 118 different items on a scale of 1 (don't like it at all) to 4 (like it very much). In addition, these same people were also asked to predict how a person with whom they shared a relationship would rate those same 118 items. Some people in the study were asked to make preference predictions for people they had known for a relatively short time (the average relationship length in this group was around two years) and others were asked to make predictions for those that they had known for much longer (the average relationship length in this group was over ten years).

The 4-point scale that the researchers employed was an important part of the study because it meant that a complete stranger completing the questions could, on average, be expected to get 25 percent of their predictions correct just by chance. Fortunately, and one suspects to everyone's relief, both groups in the study were able to predict the likes and dislikes of someone they knew better than a complete stranger could.

But...not *that* much better.

Those who were asked to predict the preferences of people they had known for an average of two years were accurate 42 percent of the time. Amazingly, those who predicted the preferences of someone whom they had known for over ten years didn't fare nearly as well, with an accuracy rate of just 36 percent.

But perhaps the most telling result of all was how little awareness anyone had of how little they actually knew about people. In the pre-study tests that the researchers conducted, both groups believed that they would be able to predict the likes, dislikes, and preferences with at least 60 percent accuracy. Of course the question to ask at this point is why.

It turns out that there are potentially several reasons why having a longer-standing relationship with another person could lead to *reduced* rather than *increased* levels of understanding of their likes, dislikes, and preferences. One obvious explanation concerns the fact that a large amount of our learning and knowledge exchanges with others occurs in the early stages of relationships, when the motivation to get to know each other is quite high. As

Skimming

VelocityReading. – Lesson 8.2 Skimming - The Spiral Technique

"The important thing is not to read quickly but to read each book concerned at the speed it deserves."

Jacques Bonnet, literary critic.

LESSON 8.2 THE SPIRAL TECHNIQUE

The objective

Again, extract quickly and efficiently the essential information:

Find the key phrases,
Grasp the main ideas,
Read the important,
Drop the extra details.

The Technique
The spiral technique, as the word inspire, is going over the text in a spiral
to get a feel and a quick overview of the content.

Again, please go slowly at first. The first time, do it with a tempo of about 10 seconds for the entire two pages. Then, to be in the right mood, count to 10, like 1001, 1002, 1003, ... and you will understand that it is more than enough time.
It is training, not racing.

Velocity Reading

Let your brain drive, and your eyes gain experience. Get used to it.

Instruction

On the following two pages of text, follow a pattern like a spiral.

Remember that the context you are using that tool is when you are having a first look at a new document or searching for something specific.

Since you are not "reading" the document per se, don't bother if you don't immediately understand what they are talking about
in the first few lines, you read.

Expect that you will probably have found the key message or phrase at the end of the spiral. However, you don't know where it is yet.

Use wide-span reading as you have learned so far.
Try to find the keywords or phrases.
You are just trying to grasp the main idea of the page.
Follow an imaginary spiral over the text like in the image here.

Skimming

Velocity Reading

Beginning of Text 1

In one series of studies by behavior scientists Benjamin Scheibehenne, Jutta Mata, and Peter Todd, people were asked to rate 118 different items on a scale of 1 (don't like it at all) to 4 (like it very much). In addition, these same people were also asked to predict how a person with whom they shared a relationship would rate those same 118 items. Some people in the study were asked to make preference predictions for people they had known for a relatively short time (the average relationship length in this group was around two years). Others were asked to make predictions for those they had known for much longer (the average relationship length in this group was over ten years).

The 4-point scale that the researchers employed was an essential part of the study because it meant that a stranger completing the questions could, on average, be expected to get 25 percent of their predictions correct just by chance. Fortunately, and one suspects to everyone's relief, both groups in the study could predict the likes and dislikes of someone they knew better than a stranger.

But...not that much better.

Those who were asked to predict the preferences of people they had known for an average of two years were accurate 42 percent of the time. Amazingly, those who predicted the likes of someone they had known for over ten years didn't fare nearly as well, with an accuracy rate of just 36 percent.

But perhaps the most telling result of all was how little awareness anyone had of how little they knew about people. In the pre-study tests that the researchers conducted, both groups believed that they could predict the likes, dislikes, and preferences with at least 60 percent accuracy. Of course, the question to ask at this point is why.

It turns out that there are potentially several reasons why having a longer-standing relationship with another person could lead to reduced rather than increased levels of Understanding of their likes, dislikes, and preferences. One obvious explanation concerns that a large amount of our learning and knowledge exchanges with others occur in the early stages of relationships when the motivation to get to know each other is quite high. As time passes, so might those higher levels of motivation, resulting in exchanges of new information occurring less regularly. Therefore, changes in a person's circumstances and situations could go unnoticed.

Another potential explanation for why people in longer-term relationships are sometimes less able to predict a partner's preferences is that long-standing relationships typically consider themselves more committed to each other by the extended time they have each invested. As a result, they may think that they know each other better than it is the case and consequently become less likely to notice changes in attitudes and preferences, especially those that occur slowly or subtly.

There is also evidence to suggest that, in some instances, people who have developed longer-term relationships may be tempted to tell white lies to each other or avoid frank and

Velocity Reading

candid conversations. The telling of white lies and the avoidance of candid conversations could serve to fulfill a critical relationship protection function and, in that context, is understandable. However, strategies that help to protect long-term relationships could lead to a decline in Understanding and a dilution of knowledge that could serve to damage the relationship. So while it might be the case that getting older may lead us to be wiser in some domains, such wisdom doesn't necessarily extend to relationships unless a process is put in place to ensure a continuous and honest exchange of likes, dislikes, and preferences with those with whom we share long-term relationships.

End of text 1

Skimming

Velocity Reading

Text 2

Could it be that even though people prefer the gift certificate with the more extended expiration date, they would, in fact, be more likely to use the gift certificate with the shorter one?

That's precisely what the researchers set out to test and what they found was astonishing. Despite participants' predictions to the contrary, five times as many given the short-expiration date certificate visited the bakery to claim their coffee and cake than those given the long-expiration date certificates. People may have preferred the offer with a more extended expiration date because it afforded them more time to redeem it; however, in reality, it caused fewer of them to do so.

As a final check to ensure that the study results were attributable principally to procrastination and not to other factors, the researchers completed a series of follow-up surveys. Those who did redeem the certificates reported an enjoyable and worthwhile experience. In addition, those who didn't convey their regret were most likely to agree with statements such as "I got too busy and ran out of time" or "I kept thinking that I would do it a bit later" as opposed to other explanations such as "I forgot," "I don't like pastries," or "It seemed like too much effort."

This research suggests an immediate small change that any communicator can make when persuading clients or customers to take up offers and proposals. Instead of offering a longer time frame for your target audience to respond, in the mistaken belief that doing so will make it more attractive, this research suggests that a much shorter

Skimming

time frame should be offered. For example, a software company seeking to boost new-user registrations might see improvements if their pop-up box is changed from the standard options "Register now," "Ask again tomorrow," and "Ask again next week" to "Register now," "Ask again tomorrow," and "Remind me again in 3 days (last day to register)," perhaps offering additional benefits or bonuses to encourage early registrations.

A financial adviser or investment manager, seeking to persuade potential investors to attend a webinar or presentation on the latest investment tips may increase sign-up rates by changing the "RSVP by" date on the invitation to one that looms sooner, rather than later. This is consistent with other research showing that email invitations indicating a specific and close deadline increase click-through registration rates by eight percentage points.

Finally, if your spouse, friend, or business partner has promised to share a fine and presumably delicious wine with you but keeps putting it off while waiting for a unique enough occasion, Shu and Gneezy would point you to a scene from the hit movie Sideways for a clue for how to potentially persuade them...

End of text 2 _____ _____

Remember or write down what you think is the main idea and proceed with the following text.

Velocity Reading

Text 3

Every day millions of customers ask themselves, "Should I stay or should I go?" when finding themselves waiting in line for a service and not knowing how long their wait is likely to be. Shoppers may switch from one line to another in checkouts hoping to pick a faster-moving one. Web users might refresh their browsers, hoping that a chosen download will run faster. Customers contacting a telephone helpline may abandon a current call and call back later in the hope that the wait time will be shorter. We might be living in the fastest-moving, most information-saturated environment ever, but we still spend considerable time waiting in line (or online).

Noting that the average American citizen can spend upwards of two years of their life waiting in line, researchers Narayan Janakiraman, Robert Meyer, and Stephen Hoch sought to identify the factors that will typically persuade people to stay in line and what will convince them to abandon the wait altogether. Their findings point to several small but significant changes that any business or customer service organization can make that could substantially improve customer retention, satisfaction, and service scores.

At the core of this research is the simple intuition that "a queue worth joining is a queue worth persisting in" is advice that is rarely taken. For example, studies have found that as many as a thirds of callers held in line when they contact a call center will hang up and dial again primarily due to pure impatience. Yet, tellingly, few people benefit from such a strategy because they typically call back at some time in the

Skimming

future, and their total cumulative wait time becomes much longer.

When viewed through the lens of persuasion science, deciding "Should I stay or should I go?" pits two fundamental human motivations against each other. On the one hand, the longer people wait in a queue, the more likely they are to focus their attention on alternative activities they could be accomplishing instead of waiting. But, on the other hand, not attending to these alternative activities could be viewed as a "loss," and—given that a fundamental motivation that we all have is to avoid losing—people waiting in line might be motivated to abandon the wait to avoid any further loss.

However, things are rarely as straightforward as they seem. A case could also be made that people who join a queue have made an active commitment, so the principle of consistency might be activated, causing them to stay put. Moreover, as each minute of waiting time passes, their motivation to keep in the line may increase the closer they get to their goal.

So in the context of this tension between avoiding loss and maintaining consistency, what do people typically do? In their studies, Janakiraman and his colleagues find that most people make arguably the worst decision by abandoning their waits somewhere in the middle. No doubt that this less-than-optimal decision will likely be accompanied by feelings of annoyance, frustration, and displeasure—hardly a desirable situation if the company that these potential customers are waiting to do business with is your company.

Velocity Reading

This prompts a question: What can be done to mitigate these feelings and reduce the number of customers who hang up before speaking with your organization? Some obvious answers would be to hire and train more phone staff or to reduce call wait times by analyzing demand and capacity and then managing it more efficiently. While all important, these seem like pretty big and costly endeavors. Given that this book is primarily concerned with deploying the smallest and least resource-intensive strategies, what else could be done? In their studies, which included several laboratory experiments as well as field data from a call center in India, Janakiraman and his colleagues tested an easily implemented SMALL BIG that showed promising results: Simply providing those in line with distractions and other essential activities for them to engage in while waiting led to a significant reduction in dropped calls. Sounds relatively straightforward, but it works.

End of text 3

Again, remember or write down what you think is the main idea.

Remarks

As mentioned earlier, use these skimming techniques mainly when
- approaching a new text, when you want an overview of its content.
- Or searching about something in a text you already read.

You will have a preference for one or two of these techniques. It is fine. You don't need to use them all.
Also, spread trying these tools over a couple of weeks so that you try them all. Otherwise, you might not learn

Skimming

which ones are ones you really can master and use more efficiently.

It would be best to try them on books you have or are planning to read for fun and test them more thoroughly.

The following is the same explanation that you already read for the X Technique.

The Objective Was
Quickly find the idea or key phrases of a page.
What You Learned
- You can quickly and easily grasp the main idea of a page just by taking a few wide-span glances.
- You don't need to read the text exactly in the same order.
- It takes only a few seconds, often less than 10 seconds, to extract the primary information from two book pages.

Explanations

As mentioned in a previous lesson, often, the author has to introduce the idea, develop it, explain it, provide arguments and pieces of evidence to support it, etc.
He will repeat himself a second time, a third time, rephrasing the message. He is trying to make sure the reader fully gets it.
(just like it is the same explanation here as one of the previous techniques...)
Because it is there more than once, the probability of stumbling on it while skimming is very high.
In this exercise it was even a little more complicated than in your usual reading:

Velocity Reading

You were not aware of what the subject was.
Usually, you will know what the book and the chapter are.
Without thinking, you will search for related keywords following the spiral pattern. Your eyes will quickly find meaningful phrases in the context of the book. It is your brain that is reading, searching...

SLOW!
If it was a little tricky, the main reason again is:
    You tried this exercise going too fast.
Because in most exercises we recommend at the beginning that you don't do it going too fast at first.
When you try a new exercise, do it slowly. It will always be easy to go faster when you master the technique.
Also, by going slow, your brain gets into the driving seat. It wants to get faster because it isn't getting enough information at the speed it can absorb.
It is much better than a finger driving your eyes ...
Understanding and comprehension are a function of the brain, not the eyes. So if you try to go faster than you understand, you will have speed but low comprehension.
The real reason you read is not to speed. It is to learn something, try never to forget that. **Speed is a tool, not an objective**.

Note
Here are the Key "messages".
Text 1
You don't know as well as you think what a person likes or dislikes. And amazingly, the longer you know that person, the less accurate your answers might be.
Text 2

Skimming

If asked, consumers will prefer coupons or gift certificates with a more extended expiration date. But, fewer will use them if the expiration period is longer.
Text 3
Keeping people busy or engaged while waiting in line or on the phone significantly reduces their frustrations.

Are your notes the same?

Recommendation
Do this exercise a few times. But, you should try it on a book you plan to read and some you already read.
Get used to:
- Take your time.
- Do not push.
- Let your brain lead your search, not your eyes speeding.
- Priority: find the idea, not the speed.

We tend to be in a hurry to ¨quickly¨ find something. Since you are using a skimming technique, you are already speeding. Therefore, let your brain dictate your reading speed for the appropriate level of comprehension.

You can use the time saved for slowing down and take more time for what you find essential.

Velocity Reading

treatment decisions could only be made if *all* the doctors contributed their respective knowledge to the group. What they found, though, was that the sharing and pooling of information rarely happened to the extent necessary for the most accurate diagnosis. As a result, less-than-optimal decision making led to poorer treatment decisions. In short, not a good outcome.

So what can be done to ensure that information is offered freely and communicated effectively? Here are four ways that you can SMALL BIG your meetings both at work and at home.

The first small change that can make a big difference is to ask those attending to submit information *before* the meeting. This may sound somewhat obvious, but its practice is the exception rather than the rule. Making this small change can lead to contributions that are less likely to be influenced by those of others. It can be especially effective for meetings where a desired output is new ideas: Asking for contributions in advance often increases the number of voices that are heard, potentially leading to a greater number of ideas generated. It turns out that a similar approach can be applied to training sessions and family meetings too. For example, when facing a situation or challenge that would

benefit from the collective input of every member of the group, instead of asking everyone to submit their ideas and suggestions at the same time, it can be much more effective to ask people to spend a few moments quietly reflecting on their ideas, writing them down, and in turn submitting them to the group. Doing this can help ensure that any potentially insightful ideas from quieter members of the group don't get crowded out by members with louder voices. The small change required here costs nothing more than a couple moments of silence.

A second small change that can make for big differences is to make sure that the person who leads the meeting always speaks *last*. It is remarkable how common it is for people who lead meetings to fail to notice their influence over the group. If a leader, manager, or a family elder contributes an idea first, group members will often unwittingly follow suit, leading to alternative ideas and insights being lost. One way to avoid this potentially unhelpful influence is to ensure that the leader solicits the opinions and inputs of others *before* publicly declaring his or her own.

Third, it can be helpful to recognize the value of a checklist. One way that physicians now routinely ensure that they avoid making

222

Skimming

Lesson 8.3 Skimming - In Columns Technique

"The important thing is not to read quickly but to read each book concerned at the speed it deserves."

Jacques Bonnet, literary critic.

LESSON 8.3 IN COLUMNS

Skimming or the art of reading the "cream" of the text. Try this technique to evaluate how comfortable you are with a pattern that is a little easier to grasp.

The objective
The objective is to
Find the key phrases,
Grasp the main ideas,
Read the important,
Drop the extra details.

The Technique
This technique is a little easier to follow because the pattern is evident compared to the spiral.
In the spiral, you had to decide how open or closed it was.
You go from top to bottom with the broadest eye span possible.
The line doesn't have to be perfect.
Again, please go slowly at first. It is training, not a race.
Let your brain drive, and your eyes gain experience. Get used to it.

Velocity Reading

Instruction

On a two-page text, like a book, go from top to bottom. Remember that the context you are using that tool is when you are having a first look at a new document or searching for something specific.
Since you are not "reading" the document per se, don't bother if you don't immediately understand what they are talking about in the first few lines you read. In the end, you will probably have found the key message or phrase.
Use wide-span reading as you have learned so far.
Try to find the keywords or phrases.
You are just trying to grasp the main idea of the page.

Skimming

Text 1

Cleverly the researchers ensured that the most accurate diagnosis and treatment decisions could only be made if all the doctors contributed their respective knowledge to the group. What they found, though, was that the sharing and pooling of information rarely happened to the extent necessary for the most accurate diagnosis. As a result, less-than-optimal decision-making led to poorer treatment decisions. In short, not a good outcome.

So what can be done to ensure that information is offered freely and communicated effectively? Here are four ways you can SMALL BIG your meetings at work and home.

The first small change that can make a big difference is to ask those attending to submit information before the meeting. This may sound somewhat obvious, but its practice is the exception rather than the rule. Making this small change can lead to contributions that are less likely to be influenced by others. It can be especially effective for meetings where the desired output is new ideas: Asking for contributions in advance often increases the number of voices that are heard, potentially leading to more significant ideas. It turns out that a similar approach can be applied to training sessions and family meetings too. For example, when facing a situation or challenge that would benefit from the collective input of every member of the group, instead of asking everyone to submit their ideas and suggestions at the same time, it can be much more effective to ask people to spend a few moments quietly reflecting on their ideas, writing them down, and in turn submitting them to the

225

Velocity Reading

group. Doing this can help ensure that any potentially insightful ideas from quieter group members don't get crowded out by members with louder voices. The slight change required here costs nothing more than a couple of moments of silence.

A second small change can make a significant difference in ensuring that the person who leads the meeting always speaks last. It is remarkable how common it is for people who lead discussions to overlook their influence over the group. Suppose a leader, manager, or a family elder contributes an idea first. In that case, group members will often unwittingly follow suit, leading to losing alternative views and insights. One way to avoid this potentially unhelpful influence is to ensure that the leader solicits the opinions and inputs of others before publicly declaring their own. Third, it can be helpful to recognize the value of a checklist. One way that physicians routinely ensure that they avoid making less-than-optimal decisions and collectively take the right course of action is to use a simple checklist. As Atul Gawande recounts in his book The Checklist Manifesto, these lists contain some surprisingly obvious but disastrous-if-missed items. Is this the right patient? Do I have their medical records? Are they allergic to anything? Do I know their blood type?

Much like pilots will employ a checklist as part of their pre-flight activity; there is a lot to be said for the organizer of a meeting to consider the essential items that should appear on their pre-meeting checklist. For example, are the right people in attendance? Is the balance of expertise correct? Is someone coming who will dissent positively?

Skimming

Finally, recent research by Juliet Zhu and J. J. Argo suggests that making subtle changes to meeting seating arrangements can affect what people focus their attention on. For example, the study found that circular seating arrangements typically activated people's need to belong. As a result, they were more likely to focus on the group's collective objectives and be persuaded by messages and proposals highlighting group benefits rather than benefits to any individual. This effect was reversed, however, when the seating arrangement was either angular (think L-shaped) or square. In addition, these seating arrangements tended to activate people's need for uniqueness. As a result, people were more responsive. They reacted more favorably to messages and proposals that were self-oriented and that allowed them to elevate their individualism.

end of text 1

Text 2

Other more recent studies have found similar effects. For example, a UK study demonstrated that people were significantly more likely to recall health messages given to them by a healthcare professional when that messenger was wearing a stethoscope than when no stethoscope was present. Interestingly the stethoscope never had to be used. In addition to acting as an effective tool to help medical professionals diagnose a potential condition, the stethoscope also effectively informs the patient of the wearer's credibility and knowledge.

Velocity Reading

Studies have shown that donning a short business suit can be equally persuasive. In one experiment, 350 percent more people were willing to follow a man crossing the street against a red light and against the traffic (and, incidentally, against the law) when he wore a suit rather than just casual clothes.

Interestingly, in all these studies, and others like them, a person's clothing primarily influenced behavior for one straightforward reason: No other information existed about the requester's expertise. The immediate implications are clear. When meeting someone for the first time, it is essential to dress at a level that matches one's true expertise and credentials. To do so is entirely in keeping with a fundamental principle of persuasion science—authority. Authority is the principle that influences people, incredibly when uncertain, to follow the advice and recommendations of those they perceive to have more excellent knowledge and trustworthiness.

But modern-day business meetings are rarely so straightforward. With the advent of different dress codes, from business formal to dress-down casual and myriad others in between, perhaps it would be more effective to draw on another powerful driver of human decision-making -similarities.

In previous chapters, we have described how one potential route to effective persuasion for a communicator is to reach out by highlighting genuine commonalities with audience members. What better way of highlighting similarities and minimizing dissimilarities than to find out the dress code of the specific organization and then match it on the day of

Skimming

your meeting? But, again, such an approach is not without its pitfalls. What if the dress code is one you would not usually choose for yourself? Are you demonstrating genuine authenticity by matching their standard? And even if you are, could the upside of similarity be a downside in that your authority and credibility could be undermined? Put more simply, is there a clear answer to the question, what is most persuasive— authority or similarity?

Unfortunately, we aren't aware of any research that directly answers this question. However, as is sometimes the case in persuasion, we would surmise that a more effective route might be to employ elements of both approaches. This could mean that, where and when appropriate, one might dress in a style similar to that of the person or group you wish to influence—but do so at one level higher. That could mean a neck tie or perhaps a jacket, for example, in an office that generally practices a more relaxed or casual dress policy.

End of text 2

Remember or write down what you think is the main idea and proceed with the following text.

Velocity Reading

Text 3

Those application letters were then randomly distributed to the interviewers who, it is important to note, weren't aware of the writing task the applicants had been asked to undertake. The interviewers were instructed to read the applications carefully, forming an impression of the applicant and indicating how likely they would be to offer the candidate a job.

When the results were analyzed, it was clear that those applicants in the influential group were much more likely to be offered a job by the interviewers than those in the vulnerable group, neatly demonstrating how the small act of writing about feeling powerful can make a big difference in the outcome.

But an argument could be made that this experiment only measured the impact of this small change in a written application. It is unlikely that people in the job market would be offered a position merely based on a letter, however well it might be written. The researchers had thought of this, too. Recognizing that a face-to-face interview is often the context in which decisions about job applicants are ultimately made, they set up another experiment where participants underwent a 15-minute interview to secure a place in a business school.

The set-up for this second study was exactly as the first but with one extra feature. In addition to the two groups who were asked to write about a time when they either felt

Skimming

powerful or powerless, the researchers added a third group as a control condition that didn't carry out the writing task at all.

Following the interviews, the recruiters assessed the applicants' persuasiveness and then indicated whether they would admit the applicant or not. Consistent with results from the first experiment, writing about a time when they had previously felt powerful had a big impact on how persuasive the applicant was rated by the interviewer. Compared to the applicants in the control condition, high-power applicants were seen as more persuasive and low-power applicants as less persuasive. These differences in persuasiveness ultimately influenced the overall outcome, and did so by a big margin.

Just under half of those in the control condition who were interviewed were accepted. For example, only 26 percent of applicants who were asked to write about a time when they felt powerless were accepted. Now compare that figure to the close to 70 percent of applicants who wrote about when they felt powerful that they were accepted.

Put a different way, recollected power increased the odds of acceptance by 81 percent compared to the control group and by a massive 162 percent compared to the low-power group.

Beyond a small change that you can make when it comes to interviewing for that new promotion or pitching to a new client, these studies have potentially significant implications for recruitment agencies and job centers, too, who could help jobseekers have better interviews by

Velocity Reading

encouraging them to consider and then write down times when they felt powerful. This might be especially important for those unemployed for an extended period. Note, too, that in addition to having people write these things down, it will be necessary to time this exercise optimally, which, in the case of a job interview, should be shortly before it takes place and not hours, or even days, before.

Interestingly, research conducted by psychologists Dana Carney, Amy Cuddy, and Andy Yap suggests another potent way to make people feel more powerful: Have them adopt a high-power physical posture. Carney and her colleagues noted that two nonverbal body language dimensions are typically linked to high or low power: expansiveness (the amount of space one's body takes up) and openness (whether the limbs tend to be open or closed). Whereas high-power individuals tend to assume expansive and relaxed postures, low-power individuals tend to take more constricted and closed postures.

In their study, the researchers told participants who came to the laboratory that the study was designed to test how the placement of electrodes at different places on the body could influence physiological recordings. In truth, Carney and her colleagues used this cover story as the rationale to ask the participants to pose in one of several different manners. The researchers found that participants who were asked to pose expansively and openly (for example, by leaning over a desk with their hands firmly planted on it or sitting in a chair with their arms behind their heads and their feet on the desk) felt more potent than those who were asked to pose in a more constricted and closed way (such as by sitting in a chair and crossing their arms and ankles).

Skimming

Even more fascinating, those asked to engage in the high-power poses were found to have elevated testosterone (a hormone related to dominance) and reduced cortisol (a hormone related to stress). This research shows how such a minor change—how you position your body—can make a significant difference, psychologically and physiologically.

Does this mean that Carney, Cuddy, and Yap recommend putting your shoes up on your interviewer's desk when you are being interviewed? Of course not. But their research suggests that you're likely to feel more confident if you do it during a phone interview or shortly before your in-person interview. That confidence might be a slight difference that helps you land that big job.

Remarks

As mentioned earlier, use these skimming techniques mainly when
- approaching a new text and wanting an overview of its content,
- searching for something in a text you already read.

You will have a preference for one or two of these techniques. It is fine. You don't need to use them all. However, they are presented to you so that you know they exist.

Velocity Reading

Also, try these techniques over a couple of weeks to try them. Otherwise, you might not learn which ones are ones you really can master and use more efficiently.
It would be important to try them on books you have or are planning to read for fun and to test it more thoroughly.

Skimming

Velocity Reading

they also "anchor" the other party, perceptually, onto the initial numerical terms. As a result, even though the recipients should ideally determine the value of the negotiated items independent of the numbers provided by the initial offer, they very often don't. They instead use the opening number provided by their counterpart as an anchor, and then they subsequently insufficiently adjust away from those numbers as the negotiation continues.

Why does this happen? Consider the case of someone selling a used car to a potential buyer. When the seller first suggests a relatively high starting price, potential buyers automatically start to think about all of the information that's consistent with that high-priced anchor point. Recall how throughout the book we have discussed how individuals are motivated to make accurate decisions efficiently. With a very high initial price, the buyer might ask himself, "Why so high?" and wonder if he needs to correct a potentially inaccurate perception of the value of whatever is being negotiated.

In trying to answer that question, the buyer is likely to spontaneously focus on the features that are all in line with the initial high price, for example, the luxurious aspects of the car, its reliability and great gas the buyer had made the initial (and far lower) offer. The seller might answer his own "Why so low?" question by spontaneously focusing on features of the car that are consistent with the buyer's low anchor—for example, that the car has several noticeable dents and scratches, the overall mileage is high, and there's an "old car smell" that now makes him wish he had showered immediately after a hard workout at the gym instead of waiting until he drove home each morning to get clean.

Because it's the counterpart of the person who makes the initial offer who automatically starts thinking about the features of the initial offer, that person is likely to start thinking that the true value of whatever is being negotiated is actually closer to the initial offer than originally thought. Accordingly, regardless of whether your role is that of the buyer or the seller, or employer or employee negotiating over this year's raise, or manager or subordinate trying to come to an agreement on resource allocation, you should consider carefully what would constitute an appropriate anchor in your negotiations and then be the first to make that offer rather than wait for your negotiation partner to make theirs. As

Velocity Reading. Lesson 8.4 Skimming - The Coil Spring Technique

"The important thing is not to read quickly but to read each book concerned at the speed it deserves."

Jacques Bonnet, literary critic.

LESSON 8.4 THE COIL SPRING TECHNIQUE

Skimming or the art of reading the "cream" of the text. Use this technique when you are skimming but want a closer look. You know or feel there is more relevant information on these pages.

The objective
The objective is to be more prudent and make sure you
Find the key phrases,
Grasp the main ideas,
Read the important,
Drop the extra details.

The Technique
This technique resembles the first lesson and the most efficient reading technique: reading with two or three eye glances per line.
The only difference is that it isn't per line but for two or three lines simultaneously.
Remember: you still are in skimming mode to get an overview.
You go from top to bottom with the broadest eye span possible. The line doesn't have to be perfect.

Velocity Reading

Again, please go slowly at first. It is training, not a race. Let your brain drive, and your eyes gain experience. Get used to it.

Instruction

On a two pages text, like a book, go from top to bottom on each page.

Use wide-span reading as you learned so far.
Try to find the keywords or phrases.
You are just trying to grasp the main idea of the page.

Skimming

Text 1

Research has long demonstrated the value of a generous spirit. After providing gifts, favors, services, or assistance to others, we become more liked, appreciated, and even physically healthier. What's more, those who have received from us typically stand ready to repay when we need something from them. This last benefit flows from the rule for reciprocation, which prescribes the willingness of people to pay back the form of behavior they have first received.

All human societies instill this rule in their members from childhood for a simple reason: It confers significant competitive advantages on a group by encouraging profitable exchanges and mutually beneficial trade-offs between group members in vital arenas of interaction such as commerce, defense, and care. In the context of a workplace environment, this means that if you've complied with a colleague's request for help on one of their projects—let's say by providing effort, resources, or unique information—then they should be significantly more willing to comply with a request for help that you might make of them in the future on a project that's important to you.

With so many reasons for being a giver securely in the plus column, it would be easy to think that a large amount of giving on the job is the surefire route to success. But unfortunately, human psychology is seldom so simple. The truth is, too much of a good thing can be harmful, even in the case of assistance. Take as evidence a study done by

Velocity Reading

organizational psychologist Frank Flynn. He examined the consequences of favor-doing among employees at a large telecommunications firm. He measured the number of favors workers did for one another along with a pair of significant implications. The first was the effect of favor-doing on the giver's social status within the organization – in other words, the giver's perceived worth to the company in the eyes of their coworkers. As you might have expected, those employees rated as more generous with their time, energy, and assistance to others were seen as more valuable. Achieving acknowledged social status in the workplace is no small feat and is a testament to the interpersonal gains that come from being a prodigious giver.

But the second consequence of giving that Flynn examined—productivity on the job —did not paint so sunny a picture. Eight measures of individual productivity, including assessments of both the quantity and quality of assigned work, showed that those employees with the highest-rated levels of assistance were significantly less productive than their colleagues. Why? Because they were so busy lending aid to others' projects that they could not pay sufficient attention to their own.

What are we to make of this state of affairs? If being a remarkably open-handed giver on the job results in high social status but simultaneously reduces one's productivity on assigned tasks, what are we best advised to do? It turns out that there is a clear answer, one that emerged from another component of Flynn's study.

It identified a small single factor that amplified both a giver's social status and productivity. That single factor

Skimming

wasn't the number of favors done. Instead, it was the number of favors exchanged. Employees who provided beneficial aid on coworkers' projects and then got valuable help maximized the beneficial effects of the giving process—not just for themselves but for everyone concerned—by rating high on both status and production. Recall that this outcome is very much in keeping with the rule for reciprocity that is vital to all successful groups precisely because it fosters mutually advantageous exchanges.

The implications of these results for each of us are clear. First, we should be liberal and proactive gibers on the job. And note the crucial importance of being the first movers in the process. Going first activates the rule for reciprocity and thereby boots the potential number of favor exchanges central to mutual success in the workplace.

End of text 1

Text 2

Sent back the same email, except in this one, expressed a great deal of appreciation. ("Thank you so much! I am really grateful.")
So what was the effect of the small addition of these eight words? The researchers found that this explicit display of appreciation more than doubled the compliance rates for the new request.

Velocity Reading

But Grant and Gino weren't done yet. They also were interested in seeing whether expressing gratitude to a favor-doer had more wide-reaching effects. In particular, the researchers asked whether expressing gratitude toward a favor-doer could increase the favor-doer's motivation to help others in general. To do this, they ran a second experiment similar to the first in many aspects: The participants helped one particular student by giving him feedback on a cover letter, and that student either acknowledged the feedback or conveyed gratitude for the input. However, in this experiment, a complete stranger asked for the (second) favor instead of the original favor recipient asking for another favor.

Again, the researchers found that the gratitude condition's compliance rate more than doubled.

Consider the significance of this finding. Simply expressing sincere gratitude toward a favor-doer doubled the chances that the favor-doer would subsequently help out a complete stranger. Additional data that Grant and Gino gathered suggests that expressing gratitude increases the favor-doer's overall sense of social worth. In other words, after receiving a signal of appreciation, favor-doers are more likely to feel that others value them.

But it is worth asking whether these impressive findings could be replicated outside the laboratory in a fast-paced, real-life working environment. Grant and Gino thought they could, so they tested these same ideas to measure how a genuine expression of gratitude might positively influence employee motivation. They chose to do so at a fundraising call center because they knew fundraising could be a particularly thankless job, often characterized by frequent negativity and rejection.

In the experiment, half of the employees went about their day usually without any novel intervention; this was the control condition. However, for the other half, the director of annual giving visited the call center and thanked the fundraisers for their work. Specifically, she said, "I am very grateful for your hard work. We sincerely appreciate your contributions to the university." That's it: no handshakes, hugs, or thank-you gifts—just sixteen short words.

The researchers could monitor the number of calls the fundraisers made before and after this intervention. Whereas the employees in the control condition continued to make phone calls at the same rate, those in the gratitude condition made 50 percent more phone calls in the week following the director's visit. Imagine the impact of this small but significant change. Even if the extra calls made mainly remained similar in terms of their effectiveness, the fact that their number substantially increased likely swelled donations.

This research highlights how much positive impact can come from the seemingly small act of communicating your appreciation for the favors and efforts made on your behalf. Although it might seem obvious, think how often you may have responded with a mechanical "thanks" without truly showing how grateful you are or providing any additional information for why exactly you've appreciated the help. Or how many times have you intended to send someone a thank-you note but never got around to it? Not only are these missed opportunities for communicating your genuine

Velocity Reading

appreciation, but they are also missed opportunities for future influence.

This research suggests that managers and organizations benefit by actively seeking opportunities to provide explicit thanks. Doing so could engender a culture of appreciation across their workplaces, inspiring other organizational good citizenship behaviors throughout their companies.

There is a potential for policymakers and civil servants to prosper from the small act of showing appreciation, too. For example, recognizing and thanking citizens for their role in keeping streets clean, neighborhoods safe, and recycling rates high could prove to be a lot cheaper than the costs associated with incentivizing those behaviors or the remedial work required when less appreciation is shown.

End of text 2

Remember or write down what you think is the main idea and proceed with the following text.

Skimming

Text 3

the reason is that when negotiators present their first offer, they also "anchor" the other party, perceptually, onto the initial numerical terms. As a result, even though the recipients should ideally determine the value of the negotiated items independent of the numbers provided by the initial offer, they often don't. They instead use the opening number provided by their counterpart as an anchor. Then they subsequently insufficiently adjust away from those numbers as the negotiation continues.

Why does this happen? Consider the case of someone selling a used car to a potential buyer. When the seller first suggests a relatively high starting price, potential buyers automatically start thinking about all of the information consistent with that high-priced anchor point. Recall how we have discussed how individuals are motivated to make accurate decisions efficiently throughout the book. With a very high initial price, the buyer might ask himself, "Why so high?" and wonder if he needs to correct a potentially inaccurate perception of the value of whatever is being negotiated.

In trying to answer that question, the buyer is likely to spontaneously focus on the features that align with the initial high price—for example, the luxurious aspects of the car, its reliability, and excellent gas mileage. Now consider what would happen if the buyer had made the initial (and far lower) offer. The seller might answer his own "Why so low?" question by spontaneously focusing on features of the car that are consistent with the buyer's low anchor—for example, that the vehicle has several noticeable dents and scratches, the overall mileage is high. An "old car smell" makes him wish he had showered immediately after a hard workout at the gym instead of waiting until he drove home each morning to get clean.

Because it's the counterpart who makes the initial offer that automatically starts thinking about the features of the initial offer, that person is likely to start thinking that the actual value of whatever is being negotiated is closer to the initial offer than initially thought. Accordingly, regardless of whether your role is that of the buyer or the seller, or employer or employee negotiating over this year's raise, or manager or subordinate trying to agree on resource allocation, you should consider carefully what would constitute an appropriate anchor in your negotiations and then be the first to make that offer rather than wait for your negotiation partner to make theirs. As Galinsky and Mussweiler demonstrated in their studies, this small act of going first could lead to significant differences in your results.

While small, it's a change that could pay big dividends. First, of course, you need to ensure that your initial offer is within the realm of reality, even if it is geared toward the limits of what is realistic. For example, it's probably unrealistic to set the initial price for your Honda Civic at $100,000, claiming that it has a one-of-a-kind scent that the buyer can't find elsewhere! But as long as your initial offer is within the bounds of reason, it's important to throw that first punch instead of allowing your opponent to do so. Failure to take advantage of such an opportunity may lead

Skimming

you to find yourself down and out within a few minutes of the opening bell.

Parents take note. Be sure you get in the first bid with those bedtimes!

Of course, we recognize that you can't always beat your counterpart to the punch.

Are there any strategies available in situations in which your opponent is the one who comes out swinging? For example, prospective home buyers must deal with published list prices before anyone even begins negotiating. Likewise, many companies tell individuals their starting salaries immediately after offering them their jobs. Fortunately, Galinsky and Mussweiler proposed and tested a relatively simple but incredibly effective strategy for escaping this psychological trap: *Focus on your idea price*, which will lead you to consider information inconsistent with your opponent's anchor spontaneously.

One easy way of doing this might be to come into the negotiation not only with your ideal price in mind but also with a written list of why that ideal price is justifiable. Even if you don't bring up every one of these points in the negotiation, simply having it there in front of you may very well be a strong enough cue to counteract the otherwise automatic process of questioning whether one's original judgment was accurate.

Velocity Reading

End of Text 3

Again, remember or write down what you think is the main idea.

Remarks
As mentioned earlier, use these skimming techniques mainly when
- approaching a new text and wanting an overview of its content,
- searching for something in a text you already read.

This Coil Spring Technique is when you want to slow down and gather more information about a section.
It might be because you feel these pages are denser with information.
Or you just used the previous techniques, like the spiral, and quickly understood this looks important.
Then you go over the page again with this technique to gather the critical information knowing that you are on an important section.
It would be important to try them on books you have or are planning to read for fun and to test it more thoroughly.

The Objective Was
Quickly finding the idea or a key phrase of a page.
Summary of what you learned
- You can quickly and easily grasp the main idea of a page just by taking a few wide-span glances.
- Following that pattern, you probably almost, if not, read the whole text using the previous wide and high-eye glance techniques.

Skimming

Explanations
From time to time, you will stumble onto pages with relevant information.

Now is the time to use all that time saved skimming: use a technique and the time to extract the critical information. Since you are still in skimming mode to get an overview or to search for something specific, you can make that coil spring more or less extended, like in the following picture.

they also "anchor" the other party, perceptually, onto the initial numerical terms. As a result, even though the recipients should ideally determine the value of the negotiated items independent of the numbers provided by the initial offer, they very often don't. They instead use the opening number provided by their counterpart as an anchor, and then they subsequently insufficiently adjust away from those numbers as the negotiation continues.

Why does this happen? Consider the case of someone selling a used car to a potential buyer. When the seller first suggests a relatively high starting price, potential buyers automatically start to think about all of the information that's consistent with that high-priced anchor point. Recall how throughout the book we have discussed how individuals are motivated to make accurate decisions efficiently. With a very high initial price, the buyer might ask himself, "Why so high?" and wonder if he needs to correct a potentially inaccurate perception of the value of whatever is being negotiated.

In trying to answer that question, the buyer is likely to spontaneously focus on the features that are all in line with the initial high price—for example, the luxurious aspects of the car, its reliability, and great gas mileage. Now consider what would happen if the buyer had made the initial (and far lower) offer. The seller might answer his own "Why so low?" question by spontaneously focusing on features of the car that are consistent with the buyer's low anchor—for example, that the car has several noticeable dents and scratches, the overall mileage is high, and there's an "old car smell" that now makes him wish he had showered immediately after a hard workout at the gym instead of waiting until he drove home each morning to get clean.

Because it's the counterpart of the person who makes the initial offer who automatically starts thinking about the features of the initial offer, that person is likely to start thinking that the true value of whatever is being negotiated is actually closer to the initial offer than originally thought. Accordingly, regardless of whether your role is that of the buyer or the seller, or employer or employee negotiating over this year's raise, or manager or subordinate trying to come to an agreement on resource allocation, you should consider carefully what would constitute an appropriate anchor in your negotiations and then be the first to make that offer rather than wait for your negotiation partner to make theirs. As Galinsky and Mussweiler demonstrated in

Velocity Reading

SLOW!
Again, speed is a tool, not an objective.
Go faster when you master the technique. Let the brain decide and drive your speed and interest.

Note
Here is the Key ¨message¨ of the three texts.
Text 1
When favors are exchanged, not just given, productivity increases, and proactive givers get more reciprocity, thus boosting the number of favors exchanged.
Text 2
People receiving gratitude tend to give more favors even to people from which they didn't receive the ¨thank you ¨ from.

Text 3
In a negotiation, the initial price suggested is used by the other party as a starting point to understand or grasp the value. The first to set that anchor, the buyer or the seller, gets an advantage in the negotiation.

Are your notes the same?

Recommendation
Do this exercise a few times. But, you should try it on a book you plan to read and some you already read.
Get used to:
- Take your time.
- Do not push.
- Let your brain lead your search, not your eyes by speeding.

Skimming

- Priority: find the idea, not the speed.

  We tend to be in a hurry to "quickly" find something. Since you are using a skimming technique, you are already speeding. Therefore, let your brain dictate your reading speed for the appropriate level of comprehension.

  You can use the time saved for slowing down and take more time for what you find essential.

only instructive when it comes to solving problems and making decisions, it can also give us a distinct persuasive advantage. For example, especially in the early stages of proposals and presentations, asking potential customers to take a step back before they consider your products and services could actually make it easier for them to subsequently do business with you.

Researchers Manoj Thomas and Claire Tsai thought that the *physical distance* between a person and the challenge or problem that they faced could influence their perception of how easy or difficult overcoming that challenge or problem would be. In one set of experiments participants were asked to read out loud a series of words that appeared on a computer screen. In front of them. On certain occasions some of the words that appeared on the screen were what the researchers described as "orthographically irregular non-words," which is scientific talk for a faux word that is made up and difficult to pronounce (e.g., "meunsteh"). At other times participants were asked to read aloud non-words that were simple and easy to pronounce (e.g., "hension").

In an interesting twist, immediately before one of the difficult-to-pronounce non-words appeared on the screen, half the participants were instructed to lean toward the screen in order to reduce the physical distance between themselves and the non-word. The other half of the participants, however, were asked to lean back so that the distance between themselves and the non-word was actually increased.

Finally, after reading out each non-word, the study's participants were then asked to rate how difficult they found it to pronounce.

The results showed that when it came to reading out the difficult-to-pronounce non-words, those who were asked to lean back in their chairs reported finding the task *easier* than those who were asked to move toward the screen. In short the experiment neatly demonstrated that when facing a tricky task, simply taking a physical step back and viewing that task from a greater distance can prove to be useful in reducing your perception of how difficult that task actually is. So next time you're stuck on that Sudoku puzzle or you're struggling to make something meaningful from the wretched set of Scrabble tiles you've picked, taking a step back and looking at the challenge from a greater distance might be the small change that

VelocityReading. Lesson 8.5 Skimming - The Zig Zag Technique

"The important thing is not to read quickly but to read each book concerned at the speed it deserves."

Jacques Bonnet, literary critic

LESSON 8.5 THE ZIG ZAG TECHNIQUE

Skimming or the art of reading the "cream" of the text. Use this technique when skimming, but you are more likely on pages where you found exciting material and need to extract more info.
It is still a skimming technique but very close to thoroughly reading the text; when you reach a section of a book, a document you know is essential. That might be after having scanned the copy...
When you almost want to read its content.

The objective
The objective is to be more prudent and make sure you
Find the key phrases,
Read and retain the important.

The Technique
This technique resembles the first lesson and the most crucial reading technique: reading with two or three eye glances per line.
The only difference is that it isn't per line but for two or three lines simultaneously.

Velocity Reading

You still are in skimming mode to get an overview of the whole document, but you know you are on serious content.
It is time to skim less.
You go from top to bottom with the broadest eye span possible. The line doesn't have to be perfect.
Again, please go slowly at first. It is training, not a race. Let your brain drive, and your eyes gain experience. Get used to it.
Instruction
As the title implies, you Zig Zag over the text.
Here we are reading one page at a time to make sure we are a little less aggressive on speed while skimming.
Use wide-span reading as you have learned so far.
Follow a pattern similar to the image at the beginning of the chapter.

Text 1

---

only instructive when it comes to solving problems and making decisions, it can also give us a distinct persuasive advantage. For example, especially in the early stages of proposals and presentations, asking potential customers to take a step back before they consider your products and services could make it easier for them to do business with you.

Researchers Manoj Thomas and Claire Tsai thought that the physical distance between a person and the challenge or problem they faced could influence their perception of how easy or difficult overcoming that challenge or issue would

Skimming

be. In one set of experiments, participants were asked to read out loud a series of words that appeared on a computer screen in front of them. On certain occasions, some of the words that appeared on the screen were what the researchers described as "orthographically irregular non-words," which is a scientific talk for a faux word that is made up and difficult to pronounce (e.g., "meunstah"). At other times participants were asked to read aloud non-words that were simple and easy to pronounce (e.g., "hension").

In an interesting twist, immediately before one of the difficult-to-pronounce non-words appeared on the screen, half the participants were instructed to lean toward the screen to reduce the physical distance between themselves and the non-word. The other half of the participants, however, were asked to lean back to increase the distance between themselves and the non-word.

Finally, after reading out each non-word, the study's participants were asked to rate how difficult they found it to pronounce.

The results showed that when it came to reading out the difficult-to-pronounce non-words, those who were asked to lean back in their chairs reported finding the task *easier* than those who were asked to move toward the screen. In short, the experiment neatly demonstrated that when facing a tricky task, simply taking a physical step back and viewing that task from a greater distance can help reduce your perception of how difficult that task is. So next time you're stuck on that Sudoku puzzle or struggling to make something meaningful from the wretched set of Scrabble tiles you've picked, taking a step back and looking at the

Velocity Reading

challenge from a greater distance might be the small change that makes a big difference.

But what about situations when these challenges concern something other than word pronunciation tasks or games of Scrabble? For example, imagine for a few moments that you are viewing a product that you are potentially interested in purchasing. Does the distance between you and that product influence how easy the buying decision becomes?

The researchers conduct another series of experiments, asking participants to evaluate and choose from various products. To closely reflect what often happens in real life, the comparisons between the different products were quite tricky to evaluate.

Additionally, it was made clear to the participants that no obvious cost benefits marked one product as a better purchase than another. Finally, the researchers varied the distance from which the products were reviewed, with some participants reviewing them close up and others from a greater distance. Immediately after examining the products, the participants were given a choice to either consider which product they liked best and purchase it there or to defer their decision for another time.

Consistent with the word pronunciation tests, the results showed that those who were told to take a step back and create some distance between themselves and the products found the evaluation task easier and, as a result, were significantly less likely to delay their purchasing decision.
End of text 1

Text 2

Imagine for a few moments that you are pitching for a piece of business with a new client and that the solution your organization offers is relatively complex but objectively the best of the available options. These studies suggest that the distance from which your proposal will be viewed could be pretty significant. Accordingly, it will be important not only to consider the content of your presentation carefully but also to pay close attention to the distance from which your content will be viewed. This might mean that instead of presenting directly from your laptop, where the viewer may have to get much closer to the screen to see what you are proposing, it might be wiser to (a) arrange for your presentation to be projected against a bigger screen, even if you are presenting to a small audience of one or two people, or (b) invest in a big-screen laptop that will allow more distance between the screen and your audience.

Similarly, a teacher leading a lesson with relatively complex subject matter such as math might find that her pupils' perceptions of the lesson's difficulty can be reduced if she arranges a greater physical distance between the students and the material. One way this could be done would be to ask her students to work standing at a whiteboard or flipchart rather than sitting down with a writing pad or exercise book. Doing so would provide an environment where it is easier for her pupils to physically step back from the taxing problem she has set in front of

Velocity Reading

them (rather than leaning back in their chairs or even getting up out of them and creating a disturbance).

End of text 2

Remember or write down what you think is the main idea and proceed with the following text.

Text 3

Retail sales staff who demonstrate products as part of a sales process might benefit from carefully considering the physical distance between themselves and their customers. For example, a salesperson in an electronics store who is demonstrating a range of cell phones might choose to retreat slightly to create a greater distance between themselves and the customer—especially at points when they are introducing relatively complex or technical product features to nonexpert customers.

All in all, these studies explain how small changes to the physical distance from which information is viewed can make a big difference when it comes to influencing perceptions and easing decision-making. They might also go some way to explain why, when agonizing over that knotty problem in the office, it's the smug colleague looking over your shoulder at your screen from a distance which always believes they can get to the answer quicker than you.

End of text 3

Again, remember or write down what you think is the main idea.

The Objective Was
Read and retain the important.

What You Learned
- You can quickly grasp the main ideas of a page just by taking a few wide-span glances.
- Following that pattern, you probably almost, if not, read the whole text using the previous wide and high-eye glance techniques.

Explanations
From time to time, you will stumble onto pages with relevant information.

Now is the time to use all that time saved skimming: use a technique and the time to extract the critical information.

Since you are still in skimming mode to get an overview or to search for something specific, you can make those Zig Zag more or less extended.

If your brain drives you, you will instinctively pick the appropriate pattern AS LONG you do it a little slower than you can speed up to.

If you are on a critical section, now is the time to reap the benefit of all the time you saved elsewhere in the document: **take your time** to absorb the content at this step fully.

Remember: you are learning these techniques to increase your knowledge and enjoy reading more.

Velocity Reading

SLOW!
Again, speed is a tool, not an objective.
Go faster when you master the technique. Let the brain decide and drive your speed and interest.

Note
Here are the Key "messages".

Text 1
Physically increasing the distance when facing a difficult task reduces the perception of the job's difficulty.

Increasing the distance when evaluating the purchase of a product increases the likelihood of making a quicker decision.

Text 2
It also applies to giving a presentation to a group, students, etc. Distance affects the perception of complexity and difficulty.

Text 3
It might apply in the retail context as well as at the office.

Are your notes the same?

Recommendation
Do this exercise a few times. But, you should try it on a book you plan to read and some you already read.
Get used to:
- Take your time.
- Do not push.

Skimming

- Let your brain lead your search, not your eyes, by speeding.
- Priority: Read and retain the important.

We tend to be in a hurry. More so when you put yourself in a context to "quickly" find something.

Since you are using a technique that helps you find the content of the text: you are already speeding.

Let your brain dictate your reading speed. It will be more effective for understanding and memory. It is how you will achieve the best rate in every context with the appropriate level of comprehension.

You can use the time saved for slowing down and take more time for essential parts you want to give it more time. **The outcome you are seeking is in the overall result.**

Velocity Reading

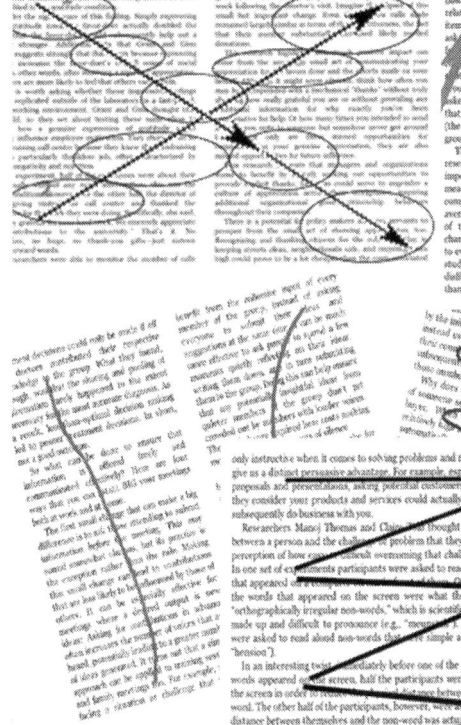

Lesson 8.6 Skimming. Summary

"The important thing is not to read quickly but to read each book concerned at the speed it deserves."

Jacques Bonnet, literary critic.

LESSON 8.6 SKIMMING SUMMARY

Skimming or the art of reading the "cream" of the text.
You learned the most common five techniques of skimming.
These are very useful and powerful to quickly grasp the main ideas of a document, a book, a chapter, etc.
The objective Of Skimming
Extract quickly and efficiently the important.
The Techniques
The five skimming techniques are:
- **The X Technique**
- **The Spiral Technique**
- **The Columns Technique**
- **The Coil spring Technique**
- **The Zig Zag Technique**

In Summary
Skimming or the art of reading the "cream" of the text.
For particular readings, it is more or less valuable to read everything.
The reasons are many:
- Too many details,
- In relevance to your interest,

Velocity Reading

- Superfluous repetitions,
- Too long explanations,
- Known topic,
- Etc. ...

Also, when you are in search mode for something specific, it is pretty useful.

Knowing the various techniques makes it easier for you. You don't have to use all of the techniques. You probably felt more comfortable with one or two of them. That is fine. Use and master the ones you like the most.

Never forget that the purpose of all these techniques is to help you read better, learn more and understand better.

Always favor having your brain, interest, and curiosity drive your readings. The brain will move your eyes and make you use the techniques to feed itself at the best speed it can absorb the information. Without noticing it, you will accelerate over useless content. You will slow down on what you feel is necessary or need more time to understand.

Consequently, you will read some text "at the speed of light ", some of it at the rate of a tortoise.

It won't bother you if you don't forget the objective of acquiring knowledge or information.

You must be comfortable overall. It will help you to reach your full potential, enjoy your skills and use them for your benefit.

Skimming

Velocity Reading

VelocityReading. Lesson 9. Tools.

"The best investment is in the tools of one's trade."

Benjamin Franklin

LESSON 9. WHY WE DON'T SUGGEST THE FOLLOWING TOOLS.

There are a few tools that are available to you.
Here are the most common and what to do with them.

The objective
When appropriate, use tools to enhance your skills.

You have or will find a few techniques
that rely on using tools or software
to help you read faster.
In this lesson, we are reviewing the most common.

WARNING
We have a bias regarding the use of these tools.

I will explain why so that you understand my bias.
Then you can make your assessment
and decide what you want to do about them.

VelocityReading.com standpoint
Most tools and software focus on speed, which is
secondary to understanding and learning.

Velocity Reading

To us, speed is a tool in support of the objective
to learn better, understand better.
And as we have written all over the place,
we recommend using your brain to drive your readings.

The objective is to learn and remember.
Not read useless stuff at the speed of light...
We suggest using these tools or crutches under
circumstances where they can help but not as primary
tools.

Always favor thinking, learning,
being conscious of what you are doing.

Example
If you start by skimming and finding the key phrases,
you might end up reading only a few paragraphs.

You might even decide that
the whole chapter is meaningless to you.

It means that using tools to pace yourself to read faster but
having to read the whole chapter isn't as efficient.

Like in the term *Velocity,* you need
the direction and the speed,
reading is more powerful when you know
where you want to go in addition to speeding.

Review of Some Other Tools

The Tools
Here are the most common tools.

THE FINGER

A finger is the easiest one to use and
you have it with you all the time ...
You will find that some books and classes suggest
to use the finger to pace yourself.
It is not a bad idea.
The problem is that it emphasizes that
you decide on a specific speed and force yourself
to keep it up by following your finger.

It will increase your speed.
I do not doubt that but:

- Your finger can't decide if you should slow down to understand better.
- Your frustration will rise when you can't keep up.
- It is disappointing when you have to slow down your finger to recover.
- It is disappointing to go back because you lost track of what you were reading or didn't understand.

Our suggestion

Use a finger as a support tool:
- To support your brain when you feel you have a hard time looking at the right places on a page.
- To mark where you would like to go back
  To read more when you are in skimming mode.
- Or when you are tired and still have to read that document, which could help you stay focused.

Velocity Reading

How
Use it as a supporting tool to help you "slow down".

Seriously.

Like when you are scanning or skimming a text.
You might tend to do it too fast.
Using your finger to point where to look and move it to the next spot might help you concentrate.
Try it.
Take a text and use your finger to follow a pattern like the Coil Spring Technique. You will probably find that when you lack interest, or you are tired, it helps.
Using a finger is cumbersome when you are focused or devouring a document.

THE HAND

The same comments apply here.
Some readers prefer to use the whole hand to go over the text to read instead of one finger or two.
It is a matter of comfort. Try both and see what you like.
The important, from our standpoint, is to remember to use it in support mode. Don't replace your brain with something else to drive your reading.

THE PENCIL OR PEN

Again, the same comments apply.
You can use it as a supporting tool when you encounter some difficulties, are tired, etc.
Using it instead of a finger isn't much better.

Review of Some Other Tools

Using a pencil or pen to take notes, underline, and add symbols, notes, and reminders to a document is very useful. It helps save time in extracting information later.

SOFTWARE

Today, with the widespread use of technology, you can buy software to "read faster".

You can look at a few applications for your phone.
You can search on Google for these.

There is one key feature of these tools.
You give them a text, and they show you the words of the text like flash cards.
It can be one word at a time or up to 3-5 words simultaneously.
You pick the speed and let the software show it on your screen or phone.
Honestly, we are not very enthusiastic about these tools because:

- Their focus is only on speed.
- As mentioned earlier, it can't decide for you to skip irrelevant text.
- However, you can try them. You will find that passing 600-800 words per minute becomes very difficult.
- Only with the first technique you learned, the "Tennis" technique where you learned to expand your eye glances, it is possible to read as fast as 800-1,200 words per minute.
- You can't read multiple lines at a time.
- You can't scan, skim and skip uninteresting content.
- You can't apply it to a book or other printed documents.

Velocity Reading

Our bias is that your brain should drive.
It will go faster, skip text, and slow down at important material.
What counts is the overall result.

Also, when you stumble on complex text or
find it very important,
you can decide to go back, read it twice, etc.

In the world of reading software,
going back is impossible or burdensome.
Rereading is a sin.

Whereas we consider that reading faster is
to have more time to learn, think, review, and understand the critical content.
Because speed is a tool, not the objective.

Even mathematically, it doesn't compute.
Reading all the words in a text, even at 1,000 words/minute, is not as fast as deciding that a text of 3,000 words is irrelevant to read or
there are only two critical phrases on the whole page...

SUMMARY

- **You can use your fingers, hands, and pen/pencil in support mode to help you focus or mark a spot.**
- **Your brain should remain the driver.**
- **The objective is to learn and understand.**
- **Keep alert to read what has value and drop the rest.**

Review of Some Other Tools

For now, we feel reading software isn't much.
We assess that it doesn't do the job so far.

The software does what it claims can, getting you to read faster. But it is in a context that is limiting you.
It's more like a crutch.

Feel free to try it yourself if you ever find one
that does a perfect job of helping you understand better.
Let us know at support@velocityreading.com.

Velocity Reading

VelocityReading. Lesson 10.
Regression & Subvocalization.

"Books were my pass to personal freedom." "What I love most about reading: It gives you the ability to reach higher ground. And keep climbing."

Oprah Winfrey

LESSON 10. REGRESSION & SUBVOCALIZATION
EASIER SOLUTIONS THAN YOU MIGHT THINK

These are qualified as reading problems.
Here is what it is all about and what to do about it.

The objective
Give you practical solutions to these two "issues ".

REGRESSION

In the world of reading, regression's definition is:
"A backward eye movement when reading a line of text. Good readers do it less than weaker readers, who go back to check things more frequently. "

Regression is often used in tests to assess
if reading faster works. In those tests,
you are not allowed to go back.

Velocity Reading

You have to read one way only.
Those who run these tests don't realize that this is tricking a test into proving a point...

At this point in this Coaching, you know
that you can read faster and better.
There is no false test that will change your new skill now.

The real problem
is partially in the definition itself.
It carries a judgment call that
those that do regression are weaker readers.

The error, in our view,
it is poorly defining
the problem.

All reasons why it happens are in the same basket.
They arbitrarily decide it is a blemish
that you must correct.

Then all the solutions are in line with that conclusion.

Regression re-visited
Unless you have brain damage,
you probably reread because
you didn't understand or lacked concentration.

If you didn't understand, it justifies rereading it,
wouldn't you agree?

About your lack of concentration, one must ask
why you lose concentration.

Regression & Subvocalization

If the answer is:

- The text or the subject is boring.
- You have no interest in reading about it.
- You don't understand it. It exceeds your knowledge.
- It is poorly written as most text.
- It contains too much text, repeats itself, is poorly constructed, etc.
- You are tired,
- Someone imposed the reading, but you couldn't care less...
- Etc.

And because of all these reasons,
you find yourself having to go back all the time
because you daydream, lose track, etc.
Using tools, software, and techniques to
force you to read that "stuff"
are skipping the observation of why
you are having a problem.

Qualifying regression as a problem when you read faster is a poorly defined problem and wrongly resolved.

Our standpoint
Regression is a natural reflex, behavior
when someone loses understanding or comprehension
of its reading.

Moreover, correctly used, it is a tool,
a strength of the human brain, <u>not a weakness</u>!

If you do it too much, there are reasons.

Velocity Reading

You need to address those reasons.
Amazingly, many daydreams during reading
and regress because they read too slowly or it is boring.
Your brain starts to think about something else
because it thinks faster than you read.

When you read to find information at a higher speed
because you can, you will very rarely regress
because you daydream or are bored.
You will come back because you missed something,
didn't understand it, which is excellent that you can,
would you agree?

When you scan and skim too fast
or skip too much text,
you can come back and go over a portion of the text
to make sure you gather the appropriate information.

So, **make regression your friend**. When you go back,
don't be trapped in the bias of calling it
regression and a weakness.

What to do
So welcome going back when it is appropriate,
it is not a weakness but an additional tool.

If it happens too often, there is a problem you need to
address. It is a warning, a flag.

Find out the real problem: poor text, subject,
lack of knowledge on the subject, etc.
And address that issue.

SUBVOCALIZATION

Usual Definition
"Subvocalization is a prevalent habit among readers.
It involves saying words in your head while reading.
It is one of the main reasons why
people read slowly and have trouble improving
their reading speeds. "

The last sentence is where it hurts.

What is true?
People that can say they do not subvocalize
say that they read faster. Guess what? It is true.

We can confirm it because
I can read fast enough in some cases
and I very well know that when I achieve these speeds
(over 2,000 words per minute), I do not subvocalize.
But...
There is a "but". Most of the time, I do subvocalize.
My usual reading speed is more in the 800-1,200 wpm
range.

90% of the time, I subvocalize.
And it doesn't bother me a bit.

Subvocalization is more a result than a tool.

Let me explain.
When you read often, are in familiar territory subject,
the author writes pretty well or
consistently give the information the same way

Velocity Reading

throughout the book,
it is much easier to read very fast.
Reading very fast and comfortably
becomes like images in your head,
a little like a movie or when people talk to you.
You don't see the words but the ideas.

That is when it happens. You grasp many words
and even lines at the same time.
You understand what it means or what it is talking about.
You are so focused that you forget you are reading.
You think about the ideas and see images in your head.
In those moments, you are not subvocalizing. It is a result.

Let your brain drive
It comes back to a fundamental principle:
"Let your brain be the driver"

Your eyes, fingers, or anything else shouldn't
determine your reading speed.
Trying not to subvocalize shouldn't either.
In our view, not subvocalizing
is not even a tool to read faster.
It is the consequence of reading better
to the point you are forgetting what you are doing.

It is just like driving your car.
Usually, you are not conscious of what you are doing,
you are focusing on where you are going.
And focusing on the activity of what you do
to drive will not make you a better driver...

Finally,

If you set a condition to achieve that level of reading, it would be like when you are going to the gym; you would try to train for the Olympics. But, under that, you would consider it unacceptable. Would that make sense? You aren't planning to win the worldwide contest on speed reading.

CONCLUSION & OUR RECOMMANDATION

Don't bother about subvocalization. Aiming at it
is very demanding and very difficult,
it is like speed for speed.

If you can go through a book
- scanning and skimming,
- Identify the most valuable chapters,
- focus on these,
- Read the vital paragraph and chapters thoroughly,
- take notes.

You will be capable of reading
an average non-fiction book, which usually contains
about 60-80,000 words within an hour, an hour and a half.

You can do it comfortably, not rushing, letting your brain assess and decide when to skim, accelerate, slow down.

When you reach such a level,
speed is not the purpose: learning and understanding are.

If you can achieve those levels of performance
and you subvocalize all the time, then who cares???

Velocity Reading

Consequently, forget about trying not to subvocalize.
It is not a tool. It is a result.
And when it happens, enjoy it.

You will be surprised and feel amazed.
But don't bother in the meantime.

P.S.
If you want, you can **subvocalize faster**. Really.

Just like you can accelerate a video on YouTube and still understand what is said. You can do it in your head.

You can accelerate your inner voice.
Try it on any phrases :)

Read what you just read above while speeding up your inner voice.
You will be amazed how fast you can read with that little voice in your head "talking " very fast...

Velocity Reading

VelocityReading. Lesson 11. Wrap-up

"The best investment is in the tools of one's trade."

Benjamin Franklin

LESSON 11. WRAP-UP

WRAP-UP OF WHAT AND HOW TO READ BETTER, FASTER, THAT YOU NOW MASTER.

Congratulations!
You have gone through all the techniques.

The objective
Revisit what you learned and remind you of a few to-dos.

Summary
You now read faster and better.
Most importantly, you now know that
letting the brain be the driver
will not only get you to read faster but
to do it at the appropriate speed,
you will learn faster, understand better,
and remember more.

You learn how to identify the quality of the content
and to rapidly focus on its core messages.

Velocity Reading

You can save time and retain critical content.

Here is what you went through

The first lesson of module one
immediately introduced you to the **cornerstone**
of this Coaching: **The Tennis Technique.**

If you were an average reader, you just doubled your speed with this technique.

It is an essential technique to read faster.
It means that on an important subject,
in a text full of relevant information, you can read
faster without skipping any text.

You learned to let your brain drive
the reading process, not artificial speeding crutches.

You got your eyes used to
reduce the number of glances per line.
As a result, you increase your reading speed **effortlessly**.

Then you moved on to lessons
to expand your vision **vertically**, which we can do.
Very useful on regular text and
smartphones or tablets.

Need practice from time to time
Reading vertically is a skill we lose a little
when you read less often or don't practice it.

I suggest that from time to time
you go back to these lessons 4 and 5
to keep you sharp on this.
It only takes a few minutes.

It will remind you how to do it,
to keep the text
a little farther away from your eyes
to make it easier.

Searching, Scanning, Skimming
The techniques of searching, scanning, and skimming
are very useful when you approach a new document
or you are searching for something specific in an old one.

There are a few techniques. You will probably never use
all of them. **Use the one you feel comfortable** with
and practice using them a lot so that it becomes easy to
use.

These techniques will help you drop unnecessary reading.
Authors usually write documents for a multitude of
readers. Your needs are specific.

You can concentrate on
what is important to you and skip
what you don't need if you know the subject,
understand it and don't need to read all examples, etc.

You don't need to read fast a text that
you don't need to read at all!

Velocity Reading

You can scan and skim two pages of a book in 10 seconds.
Then decide to move on or invest more
in that specific content. It is powerful.

You know the tools that exist
and how you can use them or why not.

Finally, there is a lot of writing about
regression and subvocalization.

Everyone is saying the same thing about these subjects
without thoroughly examining what they are.
You can use regression to your advantage.

You can forget about trying to eliminate subvocalization
it doesn't worth the effort. It is distracting.
Trying to control it is the wrong focus or objective to
have.

I hope you enjoyed learning these techniques.
You probably found most of them not too difficult.
You didn't need to invest a lot of time in each lesson.
If you practice between lessons,
you probably are very good at it now.

Do you feel that you are in control now when you read?
Have you noticed how many texts are poorly written?

Do you realize now that most writers repeat themselves?
(Including us)

They often have no choice. A book is for a multitude
and try to make sure everyone understands.
It doesn't mean you have to read everything
if you don't need to.

Now you can quickly find out if you need to read
everything,
with just a few glances.

You know now that your brain likes
to get a lot of information quickly
and it stays focused when it gets nourished fast enough.

It can understand a lot of things
with incomplete information and deduct
a lot, even before reading it.

It can read multiple words and even
multiple words in multiple lines with one glance.
(You might find this a little difficult at times, it is normal.)

To finish, I will repeat:
Let your brain be the driver.
Never forget you are using all these techniques
to learn and understand.
Speed is secondary. It is a tool.

You will achieve high speed reading
while focusing on the end objective.

I hope you appreciate the new skills you acquired for the
rest of your life…

thank you

Thank You

We thank you if you have read, learned, and apply most of the lessons in *VelocityReading*.

We are glad that you took the initiative to learn these skills

It seems even more critical than ever before.

The competitive environment in which we live is getting more challenging

Having that skill will also give you more opportunities. You can learn much more about a subject. You can read additional sources in a reasonable amount of time. You have the tools and the skills to do so.

As the author, I wrote the book to have a book to sell, but, on a different level, I was driven by a need that never went away: sharing that knowledge and skills.

This skill gives so much back, and teaching others to acquire it, is an endless need to fill.

We encourage you to give a few tips to some of your team members, family, etc.

Share what you learned with the people most important to you

Velocity Reading

PART THREE
BONUSES

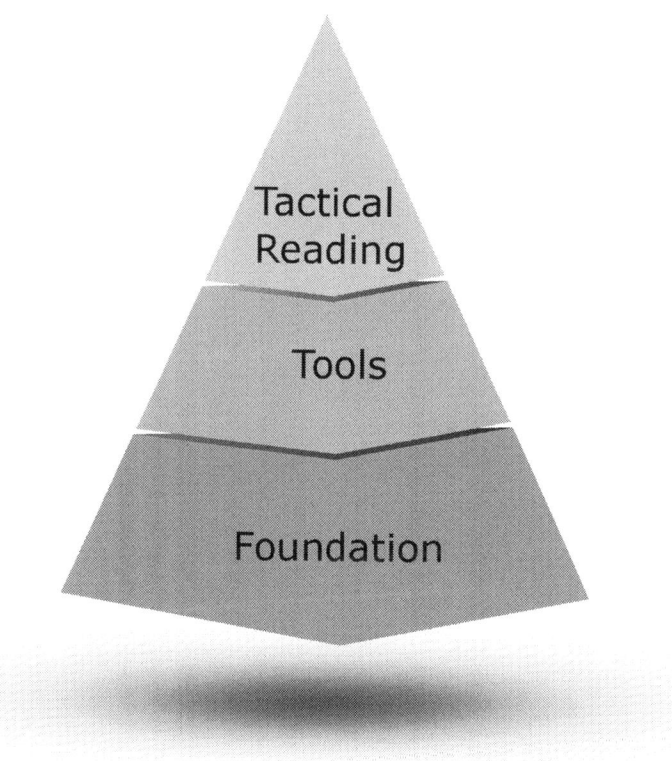

How to Plan to Read a Book

Velocity Reading

VelocityReading. Lesson 12. Tactical Reading - What is in a book?

"The most important investment you can make is in yourself."

Warren Buffet

LESSON 12. TACTICAL & ADVANCED READING
HOW TO READ A 300-PAGE BOOK WITHIN ONE HOUR!

Beyond mastering the techniques
of reading faster, there is another level
to become even better at learning and understanding

How you approach a book,
before reading it, is a powerful strategy
to learn more and much faster.

Learn to read with a purpose.

The objective

Find the most important in a book.

Before starting to read a book:

    1) Find out what it is all about.
    2) Get your mind very focused on the matter.
    3) Get hungry for learning and understanding.

Velocity Reading

Prerequisites

You will need a non-fiction book, personal development, history, textbooks... to practice—something with content you want to learn.

You can use one you already have for this lesson. The objective here is to observe what each step can do for you.

THE TECHNIQUE

The core of this technique is

> to take the time to overview the book.

We all do a little browsing of a new book.
This lesson will teach you how to do it like a pro.

Remember: **Let your brain be the driver.**
Never forget you are using all these techniques to learn and understand.

SLOW at first.

Speed is secondary. It is a tool.

> Let speed come from your brain, asking for "food" and pulling you instead of pushing.

Tactical & Advanced Reading

Instructions

12.1 - THE COVER PAGE

Read the cover page.

To show you how to do it, we will use the following book as an example here:

> The 7 Habits of Highly Effective People
> by Stephen R. Covey

Just take a few seconds to think.

Ask yourself a few questions and answers them.

Q: What do I think are the seven habits?
A: I think it certainly talks about time management, how to set objectives, to-do lists, dealing with other people, delegating, ...

Velocity Reading

Q: Why 7? Why not 5 or 10?
Q: What is the most important one?
Q: Do I have any?
Q: What will I do with it?
Etc.

12.2 - BACK OF THE BOOK

Read the back of the book.
Look for additional cues to help you ask more questions or answers.

12.3 - TABLE OF CONTENTS

Have a look at the Table of Contents.

Again, take your time, don't just go over it like you are in a hurry to go to the next step.

Study it.

The 7 Habits of Highly Effective People

CONTENTS

Foreword to the 25th Anniversary Edition by Jim Collins. 1
A Covey Family Tribute to a Highly Effective Father 9
Foreword to the 2004 Edition by Stephen R. Covey. 15

Part One: PARADIGMS AND PRINCIPLES
21

Inside-Out   23
The 7 Habits – An Overview   54

Part Two: PRIVACY VICTORY
71

Habit 1   **Be Proactive**   73
  Principles of Personal Vision
Habit 2   **Begin with the End in Mind.**   102
  Principles of Personal Leadership
Habit 3   **Put First Things First**   154
  Principles of Personal Management

Part Three: PUBLIC VICTORY   193

Paradigms of Interdependence   195

Habit 4   **Think Win/Win**   215
  Principles of Interpersonal Leadership
Habit 5   **Seek First to Understand, Then to Be Understood**   247
  Principles of Empathic Communication
Habit 6   **Synergize**   273
  Principles of Creative Cooperation

Part Four: RENEWAL
297

Habit 7   **Sharpen the Saw**   299
  Principles of Balanced Self-Renewal
  Inside-Out Again   320

Afterword   331

Velocity Reading

APPENDIX A   Possible Perceptions Flowing out of Various Centers   343

APPENDIX B   A Quadrant II Day at the Office   353

                     A Final Interview with Stephen R. Covey   363
                     Problem/Opportunity Index   373
                     Index   381

Here is what to look for:

Are there chapters regrouped within divisions?
How many divisions? How many chapters per division?
What are the most extensive chapters in terms of
the number of pages? The biggest divisions?

What does it mean? Make some assumptions about the book.
Can you figure out the book's leading content
and in which division and paragraphs?
How many and where are the secondary ideas?

What is your interest?
What divisions and chapters are getting your attention?

         Take note or remember which ones.
         Don't go into them yet, but make sure you know
         which ones. Don't hesitate to make a note or a
         mark.

Does it make you think a little more and wonder about anything?

12.4. INTRODUCTION

Read the introduction and foreword if there is. Get a feel about what the author or the writer of the introduction want you to focus on.

12.5 INDEX ... NOT JUST TO SEARCH.

Go to the index pages at the end. If there isn't, it is too bad because this is a better tool than they told you.
Be careful. You will be tempted to skip or go very fast over this. Don't.

Velocity Reading

Analyze it.

Look at the example here in Appendix 4.

It isn't structured as the Table of Contents, but it can give you insights into the book.

Look for:

>What subject have the most pages?
>If a keyword or subject has sub-keywords attached to it, what topics have the most sub-keywords?
>Do you get a feel for what it is about when you read all those words in the index?
>Are there any that are repeated?
>Are you starting to get an impression of what angle this book will be taking?

12.6 FLIP THE PAGES

Now that you have a more precise general impression of what the book is all about flip the whole book pages **slowly**.
Stop anywhere it gets your attention: titles, images, quotations, etc., and read what it is about.

12.7 SCAN AND SKIM THE CHAPTERS PICKED IN STEP 3.

You identified a few chapters you think are the most important or intriguing.

Take the time to scan and skim those chapters.

Since they are the ones you pick as the most intriguing or interesting from your standpoint, take your time.
To help you figure out how much time, you should take at least 10 seconds per 2 pages [][] that you scan and skim.
So, for example, if you want to have a closer look at four chapters of 20 pages each, you should spend about 10-15 minutes.
Very important: Take your time at this step.

12.8 READ THOSE FEW CHAPTERS YOU SELECTED

Now you can start to read that book whenever you are ready.
We suggest you start with the divisions/chapters you identified as most important and exciting to you.

12.9 TAKE NOTES.

Take notes in writing or in your head of what you know about the book now:

- What do you think is the main message/content?
- Supporting ideas.
- What seems to be the most important?

Velocity Reading

Completed

Your book overview probably took less than 30-45 minutes for a book of 300 to 600 pages.

You might have taken a little more the first time, but you will quickly become comfortable with achieving such a result with the following books.

Read

Now you can start to read that book whenever you are ready.
If you haven't done it yet, we suggest you start with the divisions/chapters you identified as most important and exciting to you.

Then continue on the rest of the book.

Or

Feel free to start at the beginning of the book and go through it as you used to. Do what is comfortable for you at this time.
It is your choice.

The Objective Was
Read with a purpose.

What You Learned

- The basic strategy on how to approach a new book, report, and document before digging and reading it thoroughly.

Tactical & Advanced Reading

- There is a lot of information on the covers, introduction, Table of Contents, and Index when you know how to "read " and decipher it.
- The 20/80 rules apply here, too: "20% of the pages account for 80% of the content. " For most non-fiction books, discipline will help you find out where it is.

Explanations

As discussed in previous lessons, the authors of books will:

- Take time to introduce its subject.
- Organize its content with the main idea
- and complementary ones.
- Introduce each idea.
- Support each message with explanations, examples, etc.
- Take into account that he is reaching various readers
- with different levels of knowledge, questions, etc.
- Will make summaries and conclusions...

He is not talking to you specifically. It is impossible. But you, as a reader, know a few things and have a specific interest in the subject. So you probably do not value that book's whole and every page.

Most readers are afraid to skip sections and miss something or feel disrespect for the author by not reading everything.

You have to know that most authors will be very pleased if they find out that you extracted the most important of his lessons, make it your own. Beyond making money

Velocity Reading

with the book, here is what they are trying to do: Give you the knowledge you can use.

No author is asking for you to read every word. The outcome they seek is a happy reader.

Example: Our Tactical Reading Of The 7 Habits Of Highly Effective People

As an example, here is what we gathered from this book.

12.1 Cover Page

When you look at the cover page, you will usually think you read the title and know what it is all about.

But this is not true. When you are preparing to read and want to put yourself in a hungry mode, the title says more than you think.

Example

The title: 7 habits... why not 10 or 5? Or only three, or the "Best Habit...", only one?
Are all 7 of equal qualities?
How many do I think I already know?

Habits? So, it does not trick, but "something "
they do this regularly... Are those habits possible for not already successful people? Will it apply to me? Will I have to change a lot of my behavior? Even ones that I like?

Effective, not efficient. How do you know you are doing the right thing? ...before you do it?
After, it is often easy, but before...

Velocity Reading

- Will that book answer all those questions?
- Where in the book?
- What would be the best habits to learn for me first?

In Short,
surprise yourself with how many questions the cover raises
for you?

It will help to put you in a very focused mode
and hungry for specific answers.
It will help you take control of the book and your reading.

The book will now look like a tool for you
to learn and find out these questions/answers.

12.2 BACK OF THE BOOK

The back of the book is often a summary of
what the author or its publisher wants you to know
about the book.

It often is a condensed or phrased version of
the Table of Content.

You can continue asking yourself questions/answers you started on the Cover page. It will also give you an idea if it is in line with the questions/answers you already started asking yourself.

Example

The 7 Habits ... the back page is a list of the testimony of well-known people that read the book.

It doesn't provide additional information on the content but emphasizes its credibility. So, I had to skip that step.

12.3 TABLE OF CONTENTS (TOC)

The first observation I gathered from the TOC is that although the book is about seven habits.

- The book has two key divisions, containing the seven habits
- The first division is for personal habits, and the second one is
- when dealing with others.
- Also, the division dealing with others has 4 of the seven habits and 30% more pages (As per the number of pages indicated in the TOC).

For each habit, I can think of questions and answers.

WHAT IS YOUR INTEREST?

Of all chapters, the ones that attracted my attention are in that order are:

Velocity Reading

1) "Begin with The End in Mind"

I know that defining the end, the objective is a good thing to do. How do these effective people do it differently than I do?
Why does it work so well for them? Why do I have a hard time translating that into a good plan? Etc.

2) "Put First Things First"

Sounds great. How do I stop procrastinating? I can't stop taking care of emails, other requests, small talk, small tasks, etc...

3) "Seek First to Understand"

Since the most prominent division is about how to deal with others, I have selected a chapter to scan and skim first like the two above: "Seek First to Understand ... "

I took note that I have a hard time with the titles
of that division, they don't talk to me enough.
It makes me think, and I am curious to find out,
what it is all about, why the writer chooses those titles,
how I will browse those sections to decide what is
essential, etc.

12.4 Introduction

In the introduction, I look for what the author is saying to get an insight into the book.

Does he talk about what it will be all about, in what order, and why?
Does he try to justify himself or use the testimony of others to support his views?
Etc.

The purpose is to help me identify what to look for first and what seems to be the most important
in its own words.

It will keep me focused.

It will also help me verify if I was right about what I found from the cover page, back of the book and the index.

Or if I need to make some adjustments to my assumptions.
I haven't read the book yet,
so I need to be very prudent in my assessment.

The 7 Habits

As an example: What I gathered from the Introduction:
- There are 17 pages of testimonies at the beginning.
- I found them a little vague,
mainly saying that it is a perfect book for

Velocity Reading

- self-improvement and changing your paradigm.
- But 17 pages confirm its popularity and widespread support.
- A foreword gives an exciting insight into
the author, recognizing he didn't come up with the ideas and that they are principles known for a long time.
- The foreword reveals those principles, more specifically to build character, are central to achieving success more than aiming at success itself.
- I found that very interesting because it raises the question, **"Is that the core message? "**.
- Since it could be the key to the book, then,
this is something I have to research first in the book.
- Now I am hungry to flip through that book to find out if I am right.
- But, continuing to extract essential information from the Introduction, I suddenly realized that
the first habit chapter is on page 74!!!
- Seventy-three pages are for the "introduction "?
- I went back to the Table Of Contents
and then effectively noticed that
- Part One ", Paradigms and Principles", precedes
the section about the three first habits.
- Because of the Title of the book, the 7 Habits... I didn't realize at first that Part One
was huge, and where did it fit?
- Now that I read in the foreword that
Principles might be the main message.
- now I wonder if Part One might contain the core message.
- The editor might have chosen the book's title
to have more impact to help interest readers and
sell the book. I wonder if these Habits, although excellent recommendations, could be the secondary or supporting

312

Tactical & Advanced Reading

messages to help implement the central message of having Principles to build Character.
- I don't know the answer to that yet. And I might be off. At this point, it serves my objective. I try to understand what is important, where to look, and on what to focus. And most importantly again,
- I am getting very, very hungry to find out if I am right and what is it the author is trying to tell us.
I am almost excited that, maybe, I read through him and his real intentions by analyzing the book's structure.
- Now, I think that I will scan and skim Part One first.
- Before that, I was more interested in reading Habit #2 Begin with The End in Mind. Because, initially, I thought that it was the most interesting. I was intrigued by what he would suggest about that. But now, I want to know
- what this Character Principles concept is. Is this the central message? Why? And where do the 7 Habits fit if that is the case? Etc.

12.5 INDEX

Pages

Here is what I gathered from the Index pages
 at the end of the book. Not for all books, but for many, it is a revealing step.
Here is what I gathered from the Index of the 7 Habits...
(For your convenience and to give you an idea of what it looks like, you will find a copy of the four first pages of that Index in Appendix 5 of this book.)
- on the first page of the index, "begin with the end in mind " is very present

Velocity Reading

- on page 2, "Circle of Influence" and communication seems important
- "Emotional Bank Account " (whatever that is?) and "first things first "
- habits are listed, but it can be expected.
- "inside-out process " (30 pages!!!), interdependence, leadership, and listening.
- Paradigm and paradigm shifts
- perceptions, Personal Ethics (26 pages), "P/PC Balance " again, whatever that is, will need investigating, and Principles.
- Proactivity, Quadrant I, II, III, IV
- Renewal, response, roles, self-awareness,
- synergy, time management, understanding,
- cooperation vs competition

It gives me additional insight into what I will be looking for and a few subjects I have no clue about, and that I should make sure
I check them even just as a curiosity.

Note: you can go at the pages and check at the same time what it is about when you stumble on something. It is part of scanning the book.

Like in my case, I went to find out what are: "circle of influence, Emotional Bank Account, the inside-out process, personal Ethics, P/PC Balance. As for everything else, it seems essential, but I assumed I have an idea at this point of what it is all about.

12.6 Flipping the Pages

Now I am ready to flip through the whole book.

My mind is very focused.
Without thinking, titles, diagrams, and paragraphs that relate to everything that bothers me
now, I will want answers
. I am hungry for information.

Flip slowly. A book of 300-400 pages can take only 5-10 minutes to flip or turn pages.
But: It will probably take closer to 15-30 minutes because I will stop and read a few paragraphs, pages, and graphics that relate to the whole preparation I just did.
You will be surprised at the results.

The seven habits...

Here is how it went for me.
I went quickly for the first 20 pages because I had already looked at it in the introduction exercise.

For the following 50 pages of Part One, I stopped and read about 4-5 pages. They were important because they were about the Character Principles, which I had identified as the possible key message of the book. (approx. 5 minutes)

I noticed a few pages talking about things I already knew so it means I can skip them or have a quick scan to make sure I don't miss anything.

Velocity Reading

Part Two, 120 pages, had a few graphics but was very easy to understand. It covers 3 of the seven habits, the ones about ourselves.

For each one, I slowed down, planning to read about 4-5 pages. I did for two of them. I just continued flipping for the third one because I felt I knew most of its message. I decided that I would have a closer look, just in case I read the book. (It took about 10 minutes).

Part 3, 104 pages, one of the four habits covered there attracted more of my attention, "Seek First to Understand ". And the examples got my attention too. I spent about 5 minutes on this one.
Remember, I am still in tactical reading mode, not reading through the whole book. So, 5 minutes of scanning and skimming was enough on a subject of 25 pages.
The three other habits, browsing while turning pages felt more like common sense and decided that I would take time for it when I come back to actually "read " the book.

The last Part, 4, is the conclusion and summary to "sharpen the saw " around good habits and keep improving. I plan to read at the end in skimming mode.

That was it for this step of flipping the pages.

It took me close to 30 minutes, **BUT**
honestly, I feel I probably have gathered more than 80% of the book. I understood:

Tactical & Advanced Reading

- The main idea is the Character Principles
- I have a pretty good idea of what he says about each of the seven habits.
- I learned some new concepts he introduced, like the P/PC Balance
- How differently does he define "proactivity"
- Begin with the end is a two-step process of creativity
- that "Seek First to Understand " is central in relationships.
- Putting first things first is the concept of focusing on essential vs urgent.

Amazingly, I believe I grasp a vast part of the knowledge it conveys after having spent about 45 minutes on it so far.

Plus, since I have extracted a "limited " amount of information, it is much easier to remember it. I am not overwhelmed with so many details that could make it more challenging to pick a priority and act on it.

IN COMPARISON

Compare that with reading as most of us were taught to read: Start at the beginning, page 1 ... In the generally accepted approach, I would probably be on page 70 at most, after 45 minutes.
I would still be in the Introduction !?!

Velocity Reading

12.7 SCAN AND SKIM THE CHAPTERS YOU PICKED IN STEP 3.

Now you go back to those chapters you identify as important.
You're getting closer to a study mode because
you know where and what is important to you.
It is worth the time now to complete extracting its content.

This step, combined with the next one
(reading those chapters)
will be the most valuable.

You can combine both techniques by reading the chapters thoroughly.

You scan and skim the others left behind
just to be sure you aren't missing something.

12.8 READING

Now you can concentrate on reading thoroughly the chapters that you decided it was essential to do so.

In total, you will probably exceed a little over an hour.

12.9 HOW TO END

It isn't the purpose of this book to give you techniques on how to remember things, but minimally I suggest you take notes. You can do that on a separate paper or on the blank pages at the end of the beginning most books have.

> The exercise of doing a summary for yourself will be of great value. Even if you are in a hurry to do something else, try to take at least 5-10 minutes to do just that.

THE END

With this approach, I went through this book of 370+ pages in about an hour and 15 minutes. It includes writing down the notes of the most important messages for future use.

> I didn't rush.
> I enjoyed it.
> I wasn't feeling pushed.
> I had the time to think about his key messages.
> I am not tired. My eyes don't strain.
> Etc.

Velocity Reading

Tactical & Advanced Reading

G ET the online version of lesson 12

If you would like to see how we read a 300-page + book within an hour, there is a course online that does just that:

https://velocityreading.com/1book-1hour

IT IS OVER-THE-SHOULDER TRAINING.
YOU WILL SEE EXACTLY HOW I DO IT.

Feel free to take the opportunity ...

https://velocityreading.com/1book-1hour

Velocity Reading

"Use all these techniques to learn and understand. Speed is secondary. It is a tool."

VelocityReading.com

Tips on taking notes
with examples

It would need a separate book to take you to an expert level. But we couldn't leave you without some essential tips
that will be of great help when you start reading a new book.

Most books have one main idea, complementary ones, supportive arguments, etc.

Before you read, decide on a few symbols you will use to identify your notes in the book or on a separate paper. Here is an example of what they could be.

ICONS AND DIAGRAMS

You can choose different ones of your own, use colors, etc.
What is important is that you can quickly know what is underlined with the symbol in the margin or your notes.

Velocity Reading

Also, suppose you will use the book pages instead of personal notes. In that case, we suggest that you write somewhere on the inside covers the cue or symbols to reach those notes quickly:

EXAMPLE OF ABBREVIATIONS
(see the application in the following sample)

MM1: Main Message #1
MM2: Main Message #2
Ellipses and boxes: choose what kind of content they are for.
Underline: Important
Double Underline: Very, very important

And add

USEFUL COMMENTS
in the margin to quickly find essential statements.

With our notes, the following is an excerpt from pages 18 and 19 of the & Habits of Highly Effective People by Stephen R. Covey

Tips on Taking Notes

inadequate, somehow "behind." No matter how much we worked on our attitude and behavior, our efforts were ineffective because, despite our actions and our words, what we really communicated to him was, "You aren't capable. You have to be protected."

We began to realize that if we wanted to change the situation, we first had to change ourselves. And to change ourselves effectively, we first had to change our perceptions.

P1

THE PERSONALITY AND CHARACTER ETHICS

At the same time, in addition to my research on perception, I was also deeply immersed in an in-depth study of the success literature published in the United States since 1776. I was reading or scanning literally hundreds of books, articles, and essays in fields such as self-improvement, popular psychology, and self-help. At my fingertips was the sum and substance of what a free and democratic people considered to be the keys to successful living.

the Problem

As my study took me back through two hundred years of writing about success, I noticed a startling pattern emerging in the content of the literature. Because of our own pain, and because of similar pain I had seen in the lives and relationships of many people I had worked with through the years, I began to feel more and more that much of the success literature of the past fifty years was superficial. It was filled with social image consciousness, techniques, and quick fixes--with social Band-Aids and aspirin that addressed acute problems and sometimes even appeared to solve them temporarily but left the underlying chronic problems untouched to fester and resurface time and again.

In stark contrast, almost all the literature in the first 150 years or so focused on what could be called the Character Ethic as the foundation of success--things like integrity, humility, fidelity, temperance, courage, justice, patience, industry, simplicity, modesty, and the Golden Rule. Benjamin Franklin's autobiography is representative of that literature. It is, basically, the story of one man's effort to integrate certain principles and habits deep within his nature.

P2

The Character Ethic taught that there are basic principles of effective living, and that people can only experience true success and enduring happiness as they learn and integrate these principles into their basic character.

Problem #2

But shortly after World War I the basic view of success shifted from the Character Ethic to what we might call the Personality Ethic. Success became more a function of personality, of public image, of attitudes and behaviors, skills, and techniques, that lubricate the processes of human interaction. This Personality Ethic essentially took two paths: one was human and public relations techniques, and the other was positive mental attitude (PMA). Some of this philosophy was expressed in inspiring and sometimes valid maxims such as "Your attitude determines your altitude," "Smiling wins more friends than frowning," and "Whatever the mind of man can conceive and believe it can achieve."

Velocity Reading

Other parts of the personality approach were clearly manipulative, even deceptive, encouraging people to use techniques to get other people to like them, or to fake interest in the hobbies of others to get out of them what they wanted, or to use the "power look," or to intimidate their way through life.

Some of this literature acknowledged character as an ingredient of success but tended to compartmentalize it rather than recognize it as foundational and catalytic. Reference to the Character Ethic became mostly lip service; the basic thrust was quick-fix influence techniques, power strategies, communication skills, and positive attitudes.

This Personality Ethic, I began to realize, was the subconscious source of the solutions Sandra and I were attempting to use with our son. As I thought more deeply about the difference between the Personality and Character Ethics, I realized that Sandra and I had been getting social mileage out of our children's good behavior, and, in our eyes, this son simply didn't measure up. Our image of ourselves, and our role as good, caring parents, was even deeper than our image of our son and perhaps influenced it. There was a lot more wrapped up in the way we were seeing and handling the problem than our concern for our son's welfare.

As Sandra and I talked, we became painfully aware of the powerful influence of our own character and motives and of our perception of him. We knew that social comparison motives were out of harmony with our deeper values and could lead to conditional love and eventually to our son's lessened sense of self-worth. So, we determined to focus our efforts on us--not on our techniques, but on our deepest motives and our perception of him. Instead of trying to change him, we tried to stand apart--to separate us from -and to sense his identity, individuality, separateness, and worth.

Through deep thought and the exercise of faith and prayer,

Tips on Taking Notes

- If you see a graphic of interest, why not take a picture with your smartphone, and keep it handy?
- Invent symbols or meaningful letters to put in the margins:
    - A: Agree,
    - D: disagree,
    - R: Research later,
    - ?: didn't understand
    - W: website,
    - Q: quotes or " " in the margin,
    - etc.

More

If You Subscribe

There are different strategies and tactics to read to learn, to teach, research for advanced school, at work, career advancement, and master your field or complementary ones.

There are also exciting paths to follow to increase your knowledge in history, economics, Business, Science, philosophy, and social issues. And you want to avoid the pitfalls of speed-reading or going through them like fast food and suffering from indigestion.

As a side benefit of being a client, you will receive, from time to time,

- ADDITIONAL TIPS on taking notes, mastering subjects, teaching, and presenting.
- REMINDERS to practice a little some of the techniques
- FREE TRAINING on some suggested skills for lack of space here.

Where to subscribe: subscribe@velocityreading.com
We will need proof of your purchase.

Velocity Reading

FREE ACCESS

In the membership area of VelocityReading.com for our customers of this book.

Send us proof of your purchase at:

freeaccess@velocityreading.com

You don't need to send it again if you already subscribed above for more tips. You will receive instructions to become a member.

- 3 VERY POWERFUL MEMORY TECHNIQUE PRESENTATIONS
    a. THE LOCI METHOD
    b. THE PEG METHOD
    c. THE LINK SYSTEM
- HOW FAST WE FORGET AND THE BEST SOLUTION NOT TO!
- IS YOUR DREAM TOO BIG?
  What Bill Gates and Warn Buffet say about it.
- A TIME MANAGEMENT TIP
- A FEW INSPIRATIONS VIDEOS
- SIX MYTHS ABOUT READING FASTER THAT DIE HARD AND THE REALITY.

Add these tips to your arsenal of skills ...

APPENDIX

BOOKS USED IN THE LESSONS
→ Links to find them online

These books are available in most bookstores and online.

You can copy the following links to find them quickly on Amazon.com

The Little Prince   http://bit.ly/the-little-prince-book

Velocity Reading

The 7 Habits of Highly Effective People

http://bit.ly/The-7-Habits-book

Small is BIG

http://bit.ly/small-big-book

Appendix ...

INDEX PAGES OF THE 7 HABITS OF HIGHLY EFFECTIVE PEOPLE

Here is an **example** of the four first pages of the index of the **7 Habits of Highly Effective People book**.
See Lesson 12 on how to use it.

INDEX

Abundance Mentality, 230–32, 312, 316
accountability, 183, 235, 238, 363
Addison, Joseph, 104
advisement response, 257
affirmation, 140–43
"Aha!" experience, 37
Alcoholics Anonymous prayer, 93
Amiel, 328–29
"Animal School, The" (Reeves), 290–91
apologizing sincerely, 207–9
application suggestions:
  for begin with end in mind, 152–53
  for first thing first, 188–89
  for proactivity, 101
  for renewal, 318–19
  for synergy, 296
  for understanding, 271–72
  for Win/Win, 245–46
Aristotle, 54
attitudes, 31–32
  definition of, 31
  sources of, 36, 38, 39, 43, 85, 131
attitudinal values, 82
autobiographical responses, four, 256–65

balance, 169, 314–15
balanced self-renewal, principles of, 299–319
Barton, Bruce, 299
begin with end in mind, 102–53
  all things are created twice, 106–7
  alternative centers, 118–26
  application of, 155–56, 158, 159–60, 177–79, 201
  application suggestions for, 152–53
  family mission statements, 146–47
  identifying center, 126–30
  identifying roles and goals, 143–45
  leadership and management in, 108–10

  organizational mission statements, 147–52
  personal mission statement, 113–16, 136–37
  principle center, 130–36
  rescripting (becoming your own first creator), 110–13
behaviors, 31–32, 98
  patterns of, 56
  reactive vs. proactive, 78–79, 84–85, 86–88, 90, 92, 94–95
  sources of, 36, 38, 39, 43, 85–86, 131
  three areas of problems in, 93
being, 39–40, 55
Bennis, Warren, 108
Benson, Ezra Taft, 320
be's, 96–97
brain, left, functions of, 138, 143, 156, 267, 287
brain, right, 137–43, 145
  expanding perspective of, 139–40
  functions of, 137–38, 156, 287
  two ways to tap into, 139–45
  visualization by, 140–43
brain dominance theory, 138, 139
Brooks, Phillips, 309
Bush, George, 274
business, synergy in, 279–81

Camp David Accord, 111
center(s), 116–36, 306
  alternative, 118–26
  identifying of, 126–30
  life-support factors for, 116–18
  possible perceptions flowing out of, 331–39
  principles as, 40–43, 130–36, 156, 179, 287
change:
  ability to, 115
  changes in, 363–64
  Force Field Analysis in, 291–95
  how to, 366–67

335

Velocity Reading

Index of
The 7 Habits of Highly Effective People

change (cont.)
  from inside out, 43–48, 327–29
  principles of, 43–48, 55–56
  from renewal, 291–95, 317–18
  role, 367
  see also inside-out process
character:
  and communication, 249–50
  three traits of, 228–32
  Win/Win, 227, 228–32
Character Ethic, 26–30, 157
  vs. Personality Ethic, 26–28, 38, 40, 197, 249–50
  primary greatness trait in, 29–30
  principles and values of, 26, 40
Chariots of Fire, 232
church centeredness, 125–26, 133, 134
Churchill, Winston, 274
Circle of Concern, 88–92, 98–99, 269
Circle of Influence, 88–99
  commitments and promises in, 99
  expanding of, 93–95, 96–97
  negative energy and, 90, 91
  one on one in, 269–71
  positive energy and, 90
  in relationships, 233
  renewal in, 301, 316, 317
classroom, synergy in, 277–79
coherence, 169
commitment(s):
  involvement and, 151
  making and keeping, 99–100, 198, 203–4, 228
  in upward spiral, 318
"Common Denominator of Success, The" (Gray), 157
communication, 25, 205
  character and, 249–50
  and Emotional Bank Account, 198–200
  empathic, principles of, 247–72
  four basic types of, 249
  from inside-out, 321–25
  integrity and, 207
  levels of, 282
  in relationships, 231–34
  synergy and, 275–76, 281–83
  third alternative in, 283–86
  see also listening; understanding
compensation system, 242–43
competition, 217, 219–20, 221, 226, 240, 241
compromise, 232, 233, 282–85, 293

computer metaphor, 78, 136, 143, 177
conditioning, 75, 78, 79, 97
confrontation, 206–7
conscience, 77, 78, 79, 136, 155, 156, 330, 364, 366–67
  education and development of, 317–18
  following, 366
  as human endowment, 77, 78, 79, 99, 107, 110–13, 137, 155, 156, 317
  in proactive model, 78, 79
  in time management, 179
consequences:
  of actions, 98–99, 131
  as expectation, 183, 235, 239, 240, 243
  four kinds of, 238–39
consideration, 227, 229–30, 267
Constitution, U.S., 114–15
contribution, as law of life, 209
cooperation:
  vs. competition, 216–17, 219, 220, 240, 241
  creative, principles of, 273–96
  as law of life, 209
  and levels of communication, 282
Copernicus, 37
courage, 211–12, 227, 228–30, 267, 296
creation:
  by design or default, 107
  first, 106–13, 136–37, 142, 155–56
  leadership and management, 108–10
  mental and physical, 106–7, 155–56
  rescripting as, 110–13
  second, 106–10, 156
creative process, *see* synergy
creative values, 81–82
credibility, 232–33, 267
crescendo, live life in, 370–71
crises, 160, 161, 162, 163, 164, 168, 169, 170

Daily Private Victory, 308–9, 316, 327, 329
daily vs. weekly scheduling, 169–70, 174–76, 179–80
Declaration of Independence, U.S., 42, 115
defensive communication, 282
delegation:
  agreements, 234–35, 238
  five elements in, 182–83, 234–35

Appendix ...

Index of
The 7 Habits of Highly Effective People

"gofer," 181, 182, 237
 increasing P and PC by, 180
 stewardship, 182–88, 234–35, 238
 in weekly organizing, 176
deMille, Cecil B., 41
dependence, 56–59, 209, 286
desire, 55, 56, 99
determinism:
 paradigm of, 78, 85, 87
 three theories of, 75–76
development, *see* growth
diagnosis before prescription, 255–56
differences, valuing, 275, 286, 289–91, 296
dignity, 42
direct control, 93
discipline, 157, 196
 as law of life, 209
 in time management, 166–67
doing, in upward spiral, 318
driving forces, 291–95
Drucker, Peter, 108, 163, 238
duplicity, 29, 206, 228

ecology, 295
education, 277–79, 306–9, 365, 369–70
effectiveness, 61–62, 108, 197–98, 295
 efficiency vs., 98–99, 105, 170, 178–79, 180
 habits and paradigm of, 55, 56, 61–62, 63–64, 67, 74–75, 99–100
 by organizational PC, 65–67
 personal, 50, 156
Einstein, Albert, 50
Einsteinian relativity paradigm, 37
Eliot, T. S., 52, 330
Emerson, Ralph Waldo, 30, 329
Emotional Bank Account, 198–200
 relationships and, 232–33
 six major deposits in, 200–212
 understanding and, 251, 253–55, 260, 262–71
 emotional deposits, 200–212
 apologizing sincerely, 207–9
 attending to little things, 202–3
 clarifying expectations, 204–5
 keeping commitments, 203–4
 laws of love and laws of life in, 209–12
 showing personal integrity, 205–7
 understanding individual, 200–202

emotional dimension, in renewal, 300, 309–11, 314, 316
emotional responses, 263
empathic communication, principles of, 247–72
empathic listening, 251–55
 see also listening
endurance, 301–2
enemy centeredness, 123–24, 133, 134
energy, positive and negative, 90–92
environmental determinism, 76
ethos, 267
evaluation response, 256–57
excellence, 42
exercise, 301–4
expectations:
 clarifying, 204–5
 in five areas, 182–83, 234, 238
 and time management, 159, 161, 178–79, 182
experiential values, 82

fairness, 42, 363
family centeredness, 120, 133, 134
family mission statements, 146–47
Farouk I, King of Egypt, 111
Ferguson, Marilyn, 69
financial assets, 62, 63
first (mental) creation, 106–13, 137–38, 142, 155–56
first things first, 154–89, 201
 application suggestions for, 188–89
 becoming Quadrant II self-manager, 171–76
 delegation, 180–88
 and four generations of time management, 158–59, 167–68, 179–80
 living it, 177–79
 moving into Quadrant II, 167–69
 Quadrant II, 159–64, 188
 Quadrant II tool, 169–71
 what it takes to say "no," 164–67
Fisher, Roger, 244
flexibility:
 physical, 303
 in planning, 170
focus:
 proactive, 89, 90
 Quadrant II, 166, 167, 169, 170
 reactive, 90, 91
Force-Field Analysis, 291–95

Velocity Reading

Index of
The 7 Habits of Highly Effective People

Frankl, Viktor, 76–78, 81, 82, 100, 115, 136, 311
Franklin, Benjamin, 26
freedom to choose, 76–79, 81, 364
Freudian psychology, 76
friend centeredness, 123–24, 133, 134
Fromm, Erich, 44
Future, 370–71

Gandhi, Mohandas K., 80, 95–96, 368
Garfield, Charles, 142
generations, in time management, 158–59, 167–68, 179–80
genetic determinism, 75
Getting to Yes (Fisher and Ury), 244
globalization, 363
goals:
 and expectations, 204–5
 long-term, 99, 143–45
 selecting of, 171–72
 in weekly organizing, 176, 177, 179–80
God, 330
Goethe, Johann Wolfgang von, 155, 313–14
Golden Rule, 202
goodness, 29, 30
goose and golden egg fable, 61
Gordon, Arthur, 304–5
Gray, E. M. 157
greatness, primary and secondary, 29–30
growth, 157
 Force Field Analysis in, 291–95
 maturity continuum as, 56–61, 118–19, 209
 principles of, 41, 42, 43–48, 55–56
 from renewal, 291–95, 317–18
guidance, 116–36, 227
guidelines, as expectation, 182–83, 234, 238, 243–44

habits, 55–56
 one, 73–101
 two, 102–53
 three, 154–89
 four, 215–46
 five, 247–72, 365
 six, 273–96
 seven, 299–319
 breaking of, 54–55
 of effectiveness, 55, 56, 61–62, 100
 of interdependence, 213–14

maturity continuum and, 56–61
organizational PC as, 65–67
readers' application of, 67–68
practicing In organizations, 367–69
relevance of, 364–66
and synergy, 61
working on, 93
Hammarskjöld, Dag, 211, 317
Handel, George Frederick, 134
happiness, 26, 38, 41, 56, 366
Harvard Business School, 32
have's, 96–97
heart, exercising of, 301–2, 304
Holmes, Oliver Wendell, 103
honesty, 42, 205–7, 363
human assets, 62, 63, 64, 65
human endowments, 77, 78, 99, 107, 110–13, 137–38, 155–57, 227, 317, 325
human interaction:
 six paradigms of, 217–27, 282
 which option is best in, 222–24
 see also interdependence
human nature, 330
 balance in renewal of, 314–15
 four dimensions of, 300–314
human relations, *see* Personality Ethic
humility, 211

IBM, 25, 98, 147–48
Identity theft, 365–66
ignoring vs. listening, 252
image, 27, 28, 36
imagination, 77, 155–56, 364, 366
 as human endowment, 77, 78, 79, 99, 107, 110–13, 137–38, 155–57
 in proactive model, 79
 visualization and, 139–43, 145
importance, in time management, 159–63, 164, 165, 166, 167–68, 188
independence, 366
 and interdependence, 196–97, 209, 217, 283
 paradigm of, 56–59
independent will, 77, 364, 366
 as human endowment, 77, 78, 79, 99, 155
 power of, 156–58
 in proactive model, 79
indirect control, 93
individual, understanding of, 200–202

Final Words

VelocityReading.com

Finally, we hope that you have acquired the skills to learn much more about any subject in much less time.

P.S. Feel free to leave a positive review on Amazon. It might help encourage a few to buy this book, learn to read better and faster and grow faster through more reading.

We will be glad if you do; it helps us. It also helps future readers. So, we invite you to be part of improving the lives of others …

Velocity Reading

Friendly Reminders

FRIENDLY REMINDERS

- STAY TUNED FOR MORE...

- SUBSCRIBE TO RECEIVE TIPS AND NEW COURSES FROM TIME TO TIME
  subscribe@velocityreading.com

- MAKE SURE YOU HAVE FREE ACCESS TO THE BONUS VIDEOS
  Send us an email if you don't
  support@velocityreading.com

- PRACTICE
  You probably use techniques like searching, scanning, and vertical reading less often. It will help you stay sharp.

- SHARE what you learned with the people around you that you care about the most.

VelocityReading.com